AGING: A guide to resources

D0872740

Edited by **JOHN B. BALKEMA**

Published by
Gaylord Professional Publications
in association with
Neal-Schuman Publishers, Inc.

Published by Gaylord Professional Publications
P.O. Box 4901, Syracuse, NY 13221
In association with Neal-Schuman Publishers, Inc.

Printed and bound in the United States of America.

Library of Congress Cataloging in Publication Data
Main entry under title:
Aging, a guide to resources.
  Includes index.
  1. Aging—Bibliography. I. Balkema, John B.
Z7164.04A33   1983   [HQ1061]   016.3052'6   83-9010
ISBN 0-915794-48-9

CONTENTS

PREFACE

Until recently the literature on old age has been minimal. It began growing rapidly after the White House Conference on Aging in 1961 and burgeoned after similar conferences in 1971 and 1981. Suddenly aging was "in," and news came from all sectors on programs and studies. A new language of gerontology was being developed; programs and services were initiated; a federal agency was mandated by Congress; and there was a general foment of activity. This activity, of course, inspired writing in many fields of study. Gradually, from this interdisciplinary literature, a core formed which could truly be called gerontology. It may be seen from this evaluation that a discipline can, in large part, be defined by its literature. In the bibliography of a subject are the basic elements of the subject and the tangential elements that enrich it.

There have been bibliographies, indexes, and abstracts of gerontology. The purpose of this book is to draw together and clarify from this chaos the tools of social gerontology—the reference tools and the working tools. The reference tools are those materials which are the armamentarium of a reference librarian: directories, bibliographies, statistical tables, and handbooks. The working tools are materials of use to professional workers, such as manuals, outlines, and guides. For students and others working outside their main field of expertise, there are textbooks and general treatises. Classics in the field are not necessarily included, but the bibliography listing the classics will be found. Only English language works are cited.

Journals that report the current literature and serve reference functions are included when applicable. The reference functions are fully described in the annotations. Because of the interdisciplinary nature of the field, articles pertaining to gerontology may be found in a wide range of journals from many specialties. Those reported here are exclusively concerned with gerontology or are from an agency or organization that deals primarily with the aging population. No attempt has been made to include popular, recreational magazines that are meant to be read by elders.

The arrangement is according to the schedule of the vertical files in the library of the National Council on the Aging. This schedule is amenable to books, pamphlets, and journal articles, all of which are included. As with any classified collection, many of the entries would fit as well in one section as another. Works on senior centers, for instance, are found under Community Organizations, but there are those who would look for them under Recreation, and a case could be made for putting them in Education. To ameliorate this problem, the indexes point the way from author or subject. The same form divisions are used throughout, so, once familiar with them, the reader can go directly to the needed section without consulting the index.

This book is the work of one hand but of many minds. It is enriched by the counsel of my colleagues at the National Council on the Aging, who represent many subdivisions within the field of aging, and of librarians throughout the country who have shared their knowledge and wisdom.

AGING—GENERAL

AGING—GENERAL

Contents

GENERAL WORKS

A1. *Aging.* Boca Raton, Fla.: Social Issues Resources Series, Inc., 1978. Loose-leaf.

A collection of 60 reprints, bound in loose-leaf form, that serves as a textbook on aging for students from the elementary to college level. The volume is updated each year with additional articles.

A2. Atchley, Robert C. *Social Forces in Later Life: An Introduction to Social Gerontology.* 3d ed. Belmont, Calif.: Wadsworth Publishing Co., 1980. 467pp.

A brief but comprehensive introduction to the subject of human aging, with particular emphasis on its social and sociopsychological aspects. There is an appendix on methodology and an extensive bibliography (pp. 397-465) covering books and periodicals.

A3. Barry, John R., and C. Ray Wingrove, eds. *Let's Learn About Aging: A Book of Readings.* New York: John Wiley and Sons, 1977. 528pp.

Collected papers introduce the reader to the many aspects of social gerontology.

A4. Boyd, Rosamonde Ramsay, and Charles G. Oakes, eds. *Foundations of Practical Gerontology,* 2nd ed., rev. Columbia: University of South Carolina Press, 1973. 296pp.

A revision of the 1969 edition, this textbook on gerontology draws on experts from many disciplines.

A5. Butler, Robert N. *Why Survive? Being Old in America.* New York: Harper & Row, 1975. XIII, 496pp.

This Pulitzer Prize winning book addresses the central problem "how does a nation alter its own cultural sensibility toward the old?", and delineates the problems of poverty, retirement income, employment, housing, service delivery, physical and mental health, nursing homes, and crime. There are discussions of politics and aging, freedom in the aging process, and ageism in society.

A6. Comfort, Alex. *A Good Age.* New York: Crown, 1976. 224pp.

Arranged in dictionary form, this book answers many questions about aging, both physical and social, and explodes many popular myths about the aging process. Interspersed throughout the book are portraits and short biographies of people who have achieved vital and productive old age.

A7. Davis, Richard H., ed. *Aging: Prospects and Issues,* rev. ed. Los Angeles: University of Southern California, The Ethel Percy Andrus Gerontology Center, 1976. 211pp.

A textbook on gerontology which gives an overview of the multiple aspects of the subject and treats six special concerns in detail. It contains extensive references.

A8. *Encyclopedia of Social Work,* 17th ed., 2 vols. Washington, D.C.: National Association of Social Workers, 1977.

Articles on all aspects of social work and biographies of persons prominent in the history of social work. The articles directly related to aging are:
   Brody, Elaine M., "Aging," pp. 55-78
   Kahn, Elsbeth, "Disability and Physical Handicap: Services for the Chronically Ill, pp. 252-260
   Piore, Nora, "Health as a Social Problem," pp. 525-541
   Hunt, Roberta, "Homemaker-Home Health Aide Services," pp. 634- 638
   Mathiasen, Geneva, "Housing for Special Groups," pp. 677-684
   Sherwood, Sylvia, "Institutions for Adults," pp. 713-719
   Perlman, Richard, "Labor Force: Exit," pp. 774-780

Kosberg, Jordan I., "Nursing Homes," pp. 1010-1017

Follett, Sally, "Protective Services for Adults," pp. 1107-1115

Pincus, Allen, and Vivian Wood, "Retirement," pp. 1213-1223

Cohen, Wilbur J., "Social Insurance," pp. 1355-1365

Schreiber, Paul, and David Fanshel, "Statistics," pp. 1611-1670

A9. Gilbert, Jeanne G. *The Paraprofessional and the Elderly.* Greenvale, N.Y.: Panel Publishers, 1977. 200pp.

A textbook on gerontology geared to the paraprofessional and designed to be used either for independent study or in a classroom.

A10. Hendricks, Jon, and C. Davis Hendricks. *Aging in Mass Societies: Myths and Realities.* Cambridge, Mass.: Winthrop Publishers, 1977. 426pp.

A textbook of social gerontology which gives an historical introduction to the study of aging, a survey of the theoretical frameworks of gerontologists, and a discussion of crucial issues impinging on the daily lives of older people.

A11. Herr, John J., and John H. Weakland. *Counseling Elders and Their Families: Practical Techniques for Applied Gerontology,* foreword by James E. Birren. Springer Series on Adulthood and Aging, Vol. 2. New York: Springer Publishing Co., 1979. xi, 308pp.

A textbook for students and practitioners dealing with some of the problems of the aging and their families. Reading lists and references appear on pages 299-304.

A12. Hess, Beth B., and Elizabeth W. Markson. *Aging and Old Age: An Introduction to Social Gerontology.* New York: Macmillan, 1980. xi, 372pp.

A textbook on social gerontology that places the problems of aging in an historical context with the prospects for change in the future. It contains a bibliography (pp. 335-359).

A13. Louis Harris and Associates. *Aging in the Eighties: America in Transition.* Washington, D.C.: The National Council on the Aging, Inc., 1981. xvii, 169pp.

Report of a poll to update *The Myth and Reality of Aging.* The present study updates the myth and reality of aging; the experience of aging; social activities and involvement of the elderly; expectations and attitudes about retirement, and preparation for retirement. There are new sections on the economics of aging and retirement; the changing face of retirement and employment after 65; social security and the role of government; and health and health care. The report includes an overview and summary, an analysis of findings with the most important statistical tables, and demographic and statistical appendixes.

A14. Louis Harris & Associates. *Myth and Reality of Aging in America.* Washington, D.C.: National Council on the Aging, 1975. 245pp.

A nation-wide survey conducted to determine the public's attitudes toward aging and its perception of what it is like to be old in America, to document older American's views and attitudes about themselves and their personal experiences of old age.

A15. McKee, Patrick L., ed. *Philosophical Foundations of Gerontology.* New York: Human Sciences Press, Inc., 1982. x, 352pp.

The philosophical, ethical, and epistemological aspects of aging and gerontology and the philosophy of science as seen by philosophers from Plato to the present time.

A16. Manney, James D., Jr. *Aging in American Society: An Examination of Concepts and Issues.* Ann Arbor: The University of Michigan-Wayne State University Institute of Gerontology, 1975. 231pp.

An overview of the major concepts in aging and a review of the important policies and programs directed at the nation's elderly.

A17. Monk, Abraham, ed. *The Age of Aging: A Reader in Social Gerontology.* Buffalo, N.Y.: Prometheus Books, 1979. vii, 367pp.

Meant for both the student and the general reader, this collection is a sample of issues, problems, policies, and services.

A18. Newman, Barbara M., and Philip R. Newman. *Development Through Life: A Psychosocial Approach,* rev. ed. Homewood, Ill.:The Dorsey Press, 1979.

This textbook for psychosocial study of the life cycle is organized around ten life stages. References at the end of each chapter.

A19. Riley, Mathilda White, et al. *Aging and Society,* 3 vols., Vol. 1, AN INVENTORY OF RESEARCH FINDINGS, 1968. 636pp.; Vol. 2, AGING AND THE PROFESSIONS, 1969. 410pp.; Vol. 3, A SOCIOLOGY OF AGE STRATIFICATION, 1972. 652pp. New York: Russell Sage Foundation, 1968-72.

The first volume selects, condenses and organizes the body of social science research on human beings in their middle and later years. The second volume interprets the data of volume one for the several professional and related fields concerned with the well-being of older people and with the prevention or treatment of problems associated with aging. The third volume, based partially on the data in the first volume, examines the broad spectrum of connections between age in general and society as a whole.

A20. Rogers, Dorothy, ed. *Issues in Life-Span Human Development.* Monterey, Calif.: Brooks/Cole Publishing Company, 1980. xi, 334pp.

Nineteen controversial issues in life-span psychology with an introduction and two selected readings for each.

A21. *Sourcebook on Aging.* Chicago: Marquis Who's Who, 2d ed., 1981. 662pp.

A compendium of material reprinted from government docu-

documents, journal articles, and other sources which presents in narrative and statistics the current status of the elderly in America.

A22. Woodruff, Diana S., and James E. Birren, eds. *Aging: Scientific Perspectives and Social Issues.* New York: D. Van Nostrand Co., 1975. 421pp.

Original articles by scientists and academicians who specialize in research and training in social gerontology. There is a bibliography at the end of most chapters.

Indexes and Abstracts

A23. *Areco's Quarterly Index to Periodical Literature on Aging.* 1982. q. ARECO, 1538 Chateauford Place, Detroit, MI 48207.

Only the first issue of this new index was seen. It indexes 40 core journals and occasional articles of gerontological interest from other journals. There is a subject index, an author index, and a book review index. Most of the citations in the issue seen were to the 1980 literature.

A24. *Current Literature on Aging.* 1957. q. National Council on the Aging, Inc., 600 Maryland Ave., S.W., Washington, DC 20024.

A quarterly abstracting journal covering the literature of social gerontology. It includes books, periodical articles, conference proceedings, government documents, and publications of private agencies and organizations. Citations are grouped by primary subject and may be found through secondary subjects and author in the annual index. Annotations are brief and descriptive rather than evaluative.

A25. Shock, Nathan W. *Classified Bibliography of Gerontology and Geriatrics.* Stanford, California, Stanford University Press, 1951. 599pp. *Supplement 1, 1949-1955.* 1957. 515pp. *Supplement 2, 1956-1961.* 1963. 624pp.

Classified bibliographies of books and journal articles in all languages which serve as an index to the literature of gerontology and geriatrics. The major portion of the work is on the biology of aging and geriatrics (the medical aspects of aging). There is a list of journals cited, with their abbreviations, an author index and a broad subject index.

A26. Shock, Nathan W. "Index to Current Publications in Gerontology and Geriatrics." *Journal of Gerontology.* v. 5 (1950)-v. 35 (1980)

Each issue contained a continuation of Shock's *Classified Bibliography of Gerontology and Geriatrics.* The bibliography did not cumulate, but there was an annual author index. From v.5 (1950)-v. 15 (1960) it was called *Index to Current Periodical Literature.*

Periodicals

A27. *Ageing and Society.* 1981. 3/yr. Cambridge University Press, 32 E. 57 St, New York, NY 10022.

A journal from the (British) Centre for Policy on Aging and the British Society for Gerontology that is international in scope. Publishes scholarly articles contributing to the understanding of aging, particularly from the standpoint of the social sciences and the humanities. There is a review section comprising book reviews and shorter notes, review articles and symposia, and a service abstracting articles from other journals.

A28. *Ageing International.* 1974. q. International Federation on Ageing, 1909 K St, NW, Washington, DC 20049.

Brief notes from member countries under broad subject headings, that give news and programmatic material, news from the societies that make up the federation, and a calendar of international conferences on aging. Other frequent features are interviews, short articles on international aspects of aging, profiles of aging in selected countries, conference reports, research reports, and cross-cultural studies.

A29. *Aging.* 1951. bi-m. Administration on Aging, U.S. Dept. of Health and Human Services, Washington, DC 20201.

The official publication of the Administration on Aging that reports on programs by, for, and with older Americans. There are original articles on subjects of social practice or of interest to practitioners, and descriptions of successful programs. It includes a calendar of courses and conferences on gerontology, projected about three months in advance; news items from the federal, state, and community levels; notice of pamphlets and booklets that may be obtained at little or no cost, and news from agencies and institutions in the private sector.

A30. *Aging and Leisure Living.* 1978. 10/yr. Modern Life Systems, 453 Fifth St, Random Lake, WI 53075.

Official journal of the National Geriatrics Society, that is an organization of public, voluntary, and proprietary institutions providing long-term care and treatment of the chronically-ill aged. Papers, often practical in nature, reflect the interests of the membership. Lengthy abstracts of theses and dissertations and summaries of research studies are published.

A31. *Aging Research and Training News.* 1978. m. Care Reports, 4865 Cordell Ave, Bethesda, MD 20014.

News of aging research and training on the federal, national, state, and local levels with reports from private agencies and institutions. Legislation is monitored and reported and trends are noted. There are reports on major research findings with contacts for further information. Grant opportunities and awards, internships and education programs, publications, mostly from government sources, are noted and addresses given.

A32. *Generations.* 1976. q. The Western Gerontological Society, 785 Market St, San Francisco, CA 94103.

Each issue, spearheaded by a guest editor, is devoted to a topic of current interest, with papers by gerontologists covering all aspects of the topic. There is a calendar and news of interest to members of the Western Gerontological Society.

A33. *The Gerontologist.* 1961. bi-m. The Gerontological Society, 1835 K St, NW, Washington, DC 20006.

Full-length articles, primarily from academia, but also by prominent practicing gerontologists. Many are papers given at meetings of the Gerontological Society and relevant symposia. Some issues contain papers clustered around one or two major topics. There are occasional supplements devoted to one topic, and the program and abstracts from the annual meeting of the society appear as a supplement to issue five of each volume. A major section of the journal is devoted to descriptive and evaluative reviews of films and other AV materials, giving source, rental, and purchase prices.

A34. *Golden Page.* 1977. bi-m. National Center on Black Aged, 1424 K St, NW, Washington, DC 20005.

News from the National Center on Black Aged. Included are short articles, many of them featuring prominent personalities; legislative news as it affects the interests of the black elderly; chapter news; reports on new programs and projects of interest to elders.

A35. *Human Development.* 1957. bi-m. S. Karger AG, Arnold-Boecklin Strasse 25, CH-4011 Basel, Switzerland.

Original papers written for professionals in behavioral and psychological development and gerontology. Papers are lengthy and most have extensive references.

A36. *International Journal of Aging and Human Development.* 1973. 8/yr. Baywood Publishing Co., 120 Marine St, PO Box D, Farmingdale, NY 11735.

Original articles on social and psychological aspects of aging, intergenerational and life-cycle studies. Each article is abstracted and referenced.

A37. *Journal of Gerontology.* 1946. q. The Gerontological Society, 1835 K St, NW, Washington, DC 20006.

Papers dealing with or bearing on the problems of aging from the biological, medical, psychological, and social sciences. A most important feature, "Current Publications in Gerontology and Geriatrics," was discontinued with the 1981 volume. This was one of the major indexes in the field, each issue listing about 1,000 publications under broad subject headings. It is still an indispensable tool for retrospective literature searches.

A38. *The Journal of Minority Aging.* 1976. q. National Council on Black Aging, PO Box 8813, Durham, NC 27707.

Articles devoted to research and other pertinent information for an audience interested in minority aging, including articles pertaining to theories and methodologies which bear upon minorities even though there may be no specific mention of a minority group.

A39. *Metropolitan Life Insurance Company Statistical Bulletin.* q. Metropolitan Life Insurance Co., 1 Madison Ave, New York, NY 10010.

Statistical articles on subjects such as longevity, disability, life expectancy, mortality, and population.

A40. *NSCLC Washington Weekly.* 1975. w. Newsletter Services, 1120 19th St, NW, Washington, DC 20036.

The journal of the National Senior Citizens Law Center, which explains legislation and regulations pertaining to senior citizens. A checklist of *Federal Register* items of interest to elders; a calendar of legislative events giving committee, place, and time; state and regional legislative news, and decisions and special reports.

A41. *Older American Reports.* 1976. w. Capital Publications, 1300 N 17th St, Arlington, VA 22209

News of events in Washington as they affect older Americans

and reports of research and studies elsewhere that pertain to topics of current interest. Background and interpretation of facts are presented in an understandable context. The style is often gossipy, so a list of dry facts can turn into an exciting story.

A42. *Omega.* 1970. q. Baywood Publishing Co., 120 Marine St, Farmingdale, NY 11735.

Papers on social and psychological aspects of death, dying, and bereavement, and other behavior associated with the end of life. Book reviews include fiction on topics relevant to death and dying as well as professional literature.

A43. *Perspective on Aging.* 1972. bi-m. National Council on the Aging, 600 Maryland Ave, SW, Washington, DC 20024.

Published for and distributed to members of the National Council on the Aging, this journal contains articles geared to practitioners in the field of aging, many of them descriptive of innovative programs. Regular departments review current federal legislation affecting the elderly and give recent news and decisions from the Age Discrimination in Employment Act.

A44. *Research on Aging.* 1979. q. Sage Publications, 275 S Beverly Dr, Beverly Hills, CA 90212.

Research papers from the broad range of disciplines concerned with all aspects of aging including sociology, geriatrics, history, psychology, anthropology, public health, economics, political science, criminal justice, and social work.

Directories

A45. International Federation on Ageing. *International Survey of Periodicals in Gerontology.* 2d ed. Washington, D.C.: 1982. 92pp.

Arranged alphabetically by country, this directory lists periodicals published within each country alphabetically by title, with some modification for the United States. For each entry it gives source, mailing address, and frequency. An index lists all periodicals alphabetically.

Guides, Handbooks, and Manuals

A46. Dangott, Lillian R., and Richard A. Kalish. *A Time to Enjoy: The Pleasures of Aging.* Englewood Cliffs, N.J.: Prentice-Hall, 1979. x, 182pp.

A book about the positive, growth-related aspects of aging. A bibliography appears on pages 169-177.

A47. Feinglos, Susan. "Searching the Literature of Aging: Gerontology Reference Sources." *Educational Gerontology* 3(1978):7-15.

A discussion of various reference tools in gerontology that lead to bibliographic control of resource materials.

A48. Palmore, Erdman, ed. *International Handbook on Aging: Contemporary Developments and Research.* Westport, Conn.: Greenwood Press, 1980. xviii, 529pp.

Developments on aging in 28 countries are covered in as many chapters, each written by a leading authority on aging from that nation. An international directory of organizations concerned with aging is appended.

Bibliography

A49. Balkema, John B., comp. *A General Bibliography on Aging.* Washington, D.C.: National Council on the Aging, 1972. 52pp.

An annotated bibliography covering monographic literature from 1967–1972.

A50. DeLuca, L., et al. *Aging: An Annotated Guide to Government Publications.* University of Connecticut Library Bibliography Series No. 3. Storrs: University of Connecticut Library, 1975.

An annotated bibliography of 220 citations to government publications published from 1960 to 1974.

A51. Edwards, Willie M., and Frances Flynn, eds. *Gerontology: A Core List of Significant Works.* Ann Arbor: Institute of Gerontology, University of Michigan—Wayne State University, 1978. xiv, 160pp.

Arranged alphabetically by subject, this is a list selected by a panel of experts as the most significant works in gerontology. There are no annotations.

A52. Grant, Ruth, et. al. *Aging Awareness: An Annotated Bibliography.* Pittsburgh: University of Pittsburgh, Western Pennsylvania Gerontology Center, Senior Citizen School Volunteer Program, 1979. 66pp.

An annotated bibliography of books and journal articles on aging in society, attitudes toward aging, elderly volunteers, curricula on aging, oral history, children's books dealing with aging, and reviews of children's literature on aging.

A53. Missinne, Leo and Bonnie Seem. *Comparative Gerontology: A Selected Annotated Bibliography.* Washington, D.C.: International Federation on Ageing, 1979. 55pp.

An annotated bibliography of books and journal articles published in the field of comparative gerontology since 1960 that are available at most college and university libraries or through interlibrary loan.

A54. Moss, Walter G., ed. *Humanistic Perspectives on Aging: An Annotated Bibliography and Essay.* Ann Arbor: Institute of Gerontology, University of Michigan-Wayne State University, 1976. 76pp.

Bibliographies about aging are classified under nonfiction, autobiographies by older authors, drama, essays, novels, poetry, short stories, and death. A list of films is appended.

A55. National Retired Teachers Association/American Association of Retired Persons. National Gerontology

Resource Center. *A Basic Reference Collection for Information Specialists.* Washington, D.C., 1980. 8pp.

A basic list of directories, readers' advisory and information sources, bibliographies, statistical publication, addresses and mailing lists.

A56. National Retired Teachers Association/American Association of Retired Persons. National Gerontology Resource Center. *Introductory Readings in Social Gerontology: A Selective Annotated Bibliography.* Washington, D.C., 1981. 11pp.

A selected, annotated bibliography of 40 citations including textbooks, anthologies, film guides, statistical resources, selected classics and books written to help elders adjust to and enjoy the experiences of aging.

A57. National Retired Teachers Association/American Association of Retired Persons. *Learning About Aging.* Chicago: American Library Association, 1981. vi, 64pp.

A bibliography designed to help educators who are introducing the topic of aging to students and to aid in locating material for curriculum development and for classroom use. There are 120 books and 33 audiovisual items cited and annotated, with suggestions for use. Subject and author/title indexes.

A58. Place, Linna Funk, Linda Parker, and Forrest J. Berghorn. *Aged and Aging: An Annotated Bibliography and Library Research Guide.* Boulder, Colo.: Westview Press, 1981. xi, 128pp.

An annotated bibliography of books and journal articles designed to introduce undergraduates to library research in the field of gerontology. There is a reference section listing general reference books, topical bibliographies, handbooks, directories, journals, organizations concerned with aging, and government agencies, followed by citations under topical subject headings. Author and title indexes.

A59. Rook, M. Leigh, and C. Ray Wingrove. *Gerontology: An Annotated Bibliography.* Washington, D.C.: University Press of America, 1977. 262pp.

An annotated bibliography of the work on aging, exclusive of journal literature, published from 1966 to 1977. Citations are arranged under 33 headings followed by a list of journals in the field and an author index.

A60. Sharma, Prakash C. *Aging and Communication: A Selected Bibliographic Research Guide,* Pts. 1 and 2. Public Administration Series No. P 69 and 70. Monticello, Ill.: Vance Bibliographies, 1978. 8+10pp.

Bibliographies listing both books and journal articles alphabetically by author. The first part covers the literature 1950-1970 and the second part covers 1971-1975.

A61. U.S. Administration on Aging. *More Words on Aging: A Bibliography of Selected 1968–1970 References.* Washington, D.C.: U.S. Government Printing Office, 1971, vi, 107pp.

A supplement to *Words on Aging* covering books, journal articles, and pamphlets published from 1968 through 1970. It was prepared for the White House Conference on Aging in 1971.

A62. U.S. Administration on Aging. *Words on Aging: A Bibliography of Selected Annotated References.* Washington, D.C.: U.S. Government Printing Office, 1970. vi, 190pp.

A general, classified annotated bibliography on aging prepared to update but not supersede *Aging in the Modern World.* It lists periodical articles from 1963 through 1967 and selected books from 1900 through 1967. Legislation is not covered.

A63. U.S. Department of Health, Education, and Welfare. Library. *Selected References on Aging: An Annotated Bibliography.* Washington, D.C.: U.S. Government Printing Office, 1959. vi, 110pp.

A classified annotated bibliography of books and journal articles chosen to give a broad perspective of the field of aging. It was issued in preparation for the White House Conference on Aging in 1961.

A64. U.S. Office of Aging. *Aging in the Modern World: An Annotated Bibliography.* Washington, D.C.: U.S. Government Printing Office, 1963. 194pp.

A general, classified, annotated bibliography on aging, prepared to complement *Selected References on Aging.* It cites books published between 1900 and 1963 and journal articles from 1958 to 1963.

STATISTICS

A65. American Council of Life Insurance. *Work, Leisure and Retirement.* Data Track, No. 3. New York: 1976. 45pp.

Data Track is a series of reports that compile and interpret statistical information of direct concern to life insurance executives. This volume contains statistics on work, leisure, and retirement.

A66. Brotman, Herman B. *Every Ninth American.* Washington, D.C.: U.S. Government Printing Office, 1980. 23pp.

A statistical report prepared for the Special Committee on Aging, United States Senate. Economic, health, housing, and social characteristics are given in narrative as well as tabular form. Population statistics are given by state.

A67. Harris, Charles S., ed. *Fact Book on Aging: A Profile of America's Older Population.* Washington, D.C.: National Council on the Aging, 1978. viii, 263pp.

Extensive current data in eight areas of aging—demography, income, employment, physical and mental health, housing, transportation, and crime victimization. Tables, charts, and a bibliography are included in each chapter.

A68. Research and Forecasts. *Report on Aging in America: Trials and Triumphs.* Monticello, Ill.: American Healthcare Corporation, 1980. 105pp.

A study of physical activity, patterns of socialization, sense of optimism, sense of financial stress, self-perceived health, frequency of religious attendance, and other behavioral and attitudinal characteristics correlated with coping with financial stress, health problems, and being alone. The study is profusely illustrated with charts and graphs.

A69. U.S. Bureau of the Census. Social and Economic Characteristics of the Older Population: 1978. *Current Population Reports,* Series P-23, *Special Studies* No. 85 (1979) 44pp.

Charts and detailed tables on aging aspects of population, family, institutional care, nativity, mobility, education, voting and registration, labor force participation, employment status, occupation, income and earnings, poverty status, housing, health and health services, and crime victimization.

A70. White House Conference on Aging, 1981. *Chartbook on Aging in America.* Comp. by Carole Allan and Herman Brotman. Washington, D.C., 1981. 141pp.

Prepared for the participants in the 1981 White House Conference on Aging, this multi-colored chartbook shows demographic, economic and other developments—past, present and projected. For each page of text there is a page of unusually clear charts and graphs. Material is arranged under seven large categories.

Guides, Handbooks and Manuals

A71. U.S. Bureau of the Census. *Guide to Census Data on the Elderly.* Washington, D.C.: U.S. Government Printing Office, 1978. 74pp.

This study, made under interagency agreement between the Bureau and Administration on Aging, is a guide to data on the elderly available from the *1970 Census of Population and Housing* and some available data from selected annual surveys conducted since the 1970 census.

A72. U.S. Interdepartmental Working Group on Aging. *Inventory of Federal Statistical Programs Relating to Older Persons.* Washington, D.C.: U.S. National Clearinghouse on Aging, 1979. iii, 113pp.

An attempt to gather in one place information on all federal surveys and programs containing data related to the elderly population. Arranged alphabetically by agency or department, data for each program include name, purpose, scope and method of data collection, limitations and reliability of data, lowest level of geography, age detail, frequency of data collection, method of data storage, availability of unpublished data, time lag of data, publication program, contact person. There is an index of data items.

YEARBOOKS

A73. *Annual Review of Gerontology and Geriatrics,* Vol. I. New York: Springer Publishing Co., 1980.

The first volume in a series of annual reviews designed to encompass the broad spectrum of concerns in aging, from empirical and theoretical literature to clinical studies and services for the elderly.

AUDIOVISUAL MATERIALS

A74. *Educational Film Locator of the Consortium of University Film Centers and the R.R. Bowker Co.* New York: R.R. Bowker, 1978. 2178pp.

A union list of titles held by member libraries and a compilation and standardization of their fifty separate catalogs, representing about 200,000 film holdings with their geographic locations. The titles are listed by subject, title, and audience level.

A75. Hirschfield, Ira S., and Theresa M. Lambert. *Audio-Visual Aids: Uses and Resources in Gerontology*. Los Angeles: The University of Southern California Press, 1978. iii, 179pp.

Information on how to find, select, utilize, and evaluate audiovisual aids to enhance the development of gerontological curricula.

A76. Sahara, Penelope, comp. *Media Resources for Gerontology*. Ann Arbor: University of Michigan, Institute of Gerontology. 1977. xii, 144pp.

Films, filmstrips, slides, videotapes, and audiotapes are described and indexed. Each entry gives title, duration, color, date, description, and source for rental or purchase.

A77. Southern California, University of. Ethel Percy Andrus Gerontology Center. *About Aging: A Catalog of Films*, 4th ed., comp. Mildred V. Allyn. Los Angeles: 1979. vi, 249pp.

A catalog of over 600 films and videocassettes. The films are listed alphabetically, and a subject index is included. Each citation gives title, technical information, descriptive annotations, producer, availability, and distributor. A list of distributors with addresses and phone numbers is appended.

A78. _____. *About Aging: A Catalog of Films*, supplement to the 4th ed., comp. Mildred V. Allyn. Los Angeles, 1981. v, 100pp.

Over 200 citations supplement the fourth edition of this film catalog. Video materials are interfiled with films.

History

A79. Achenbaum, W. Andrew. *Old Age in the New Land: The American Experience Since 1790*. Baltimore: Johns Hopkins University Press, 1978. xii, 234pp.

A history of aging in America that emphasizes the interplay of cultural trends and structural patterns in shaping the perceived meanings and the actual experience of being old. It contains a bibliography (pp. 219–228).

A80. Calhoun, Richard B. *In Search of the New Old: Redefining Old Age in America, 1945- 1970.* New York: Elsevier, 1978. v, 280pp.

A history of the reformist groups, active after World War II, which contributed to the renovation of the popular conception of the later years of life.

A81. Fischer, David Hackett. *Growing Old in America.* (The Bland-Lee Lectures delivered at Clark University.) New York: Oxford University Press, 1977. 242pp.

A social history of old age in America from colonial times to the present.

A82. Freeman, Joseph T. *Aging: Its History and Literature.* New York: Human Sciences Press, 1979. 161pp.

Materials for the history of gerontology, primarily from a medical point of view. A brief outline of the history of gerontology from the beginning of historic time, a list of one hundred distinguished works, a classified bibliography of the historians of gerontology in the twentieth century, and a classified list of journals is given.

Bibliography

A83. Conrad, James H. *An Annotated Bibliography of the History of Old Age in America.* (Center for Studies in Aging Series, No. 8) Denton: North Texas State University, Center for Studies in Aging, 1978. ix, 31pp.

An alphabetical bibliography of 152 books, journal articles, and government documents on the history of old age in America. There are subject and chronological indices.

TESTING

A84. George, Linda K., and Lucille B. Bearon. *Quality of Life in Older Persons: Meaning and Measurement.* New York: Human Sciences Press, 1980. xii, 238pp.

A conceptual context is presented for the assessment of the quality of life; a set of criteria is introduced to use in selecting a measuring instrument; twenty-two measuring instruments are described and evaluated in terms of psychometric properties and conceptual and methodological issues. A bibliography appears on pages 203-229.

A85. *Research Instruments in Social Gerontology,* Vol. 1, *Clinical and Social Psychology.* Ed. by David J. Mangen and Warren A. Peterson. Minneapolis: University of Minnesota Press, 1982. xiv, 652pp.

The first of a three volume series assessing the instruments used in the field of aging. Each chapter gives a narrative review of the major theoretical concerns and measurement strategies; a collection of abstracts, each with a conceptual definition and description of a specific instrument together with data about samples, reliability, validity, scaling properties and correlations with age; and, whenever possible, the instruments themselves.

DEMOGRAPHY

A86. Fowler, Donald F. *Some Prospects for the Future Elderly Population.* (Statistical Reports on Older Americans, No. 3.) Washington, D.C.: U.S. National Clearinghouse on Aging, 1978. 16pp.

Demographic, social and economic projections for the aging population.

A87. "Projections of the Population of the United States: 1977 to 2050." *Current Population Reports.* Series P-25, (July 1977), No. 704, 87pp.

Tables presenting projections of the United States population by age and sex and of the components of population change (births, deaths and migration).

A88. Soldo, Beth J. "America's Elderly in the 1980s." *Population Bulletin,* Vol. 35, No. 4, (November 1980): entire issue.

Statistical figures and tables on today's elderly. Extensive references and a selected bibliography are included.

A89. U.S. Bureau of the Census. "Illustrated Projections of State Population by Age, Race, and Sex: 1975 to 2000." *Current Population Reports.* Series P-25, No. 796 (1979).

Projections of total population by states, in five-year increments by race, sex, and age; population migration into and out of states by race and age and other detailed tables where age is not a variable.

A90. U.S. Bureau of the Census. "Population Profile of the United States: 1974." *Current Population Reports. Population Characteristics.* Series P-20, No. 279 (March 1975).

Statistical tables on population growth, social characteristics, distribution, employment, and income and ethnic groups. Many of the tables have a breakdown by age.

A91. U.S. Bureau of the Census. "Projections of the Population of the United States: 1975 to 2050." *Current Population Reports.* Series P-25, No. 610 (October 1975). 143pp.

Annual population projections from 1975 to 2050 by age, sex, and race. Tables include estimates for many variables such as mortality, fertility, and immigration.

Bibliography

A92. Reeves, Pamela W. *Retirement Migration: A Bibliography.* Council of Planning Libraries Exchange Bibliography No. 1510. Monticello, Ill.: Council of Planning Librarians, 1978. 11pp.

A classified bibliography on migration by older people which includes books, journals, government reports, and papers.

FUTURE ASPECTS

A93. Clark, Robert, and Joseph Spengler. "Population Aging in the Twenty-First Century." *Aging*. 279-280 (January-February 1978):6-13.

A profile of the elderly population in the first half of the twenty-first century.

A94. Jarvik, Lissy F., ed. *Aging into the 21st Century: Middle-Agers Today*. New York, Gardner Press, 1978. Distributed by Halsted Press, division of John Wiley & Sons. ix, 214pp.

Experts from many fields discuss the future in terms of the aging population.

A95. Peterson, David A., Chuck Powell, and Lawrie Robertson. "Aging in America: Toward the Year 2000." *The Gerontologist*. 16 (June 1976):264-270.

Covers a number of trends that may influence the field of aging in the next 25 years. The article contains extensive references.

A96. Spengler, Joseph J. *Facing Zero Population Growth: Reactions and Interpretations, Past and Present*. Durham, N.C.: Duke University Press, 1978. xiv, 288pp.

A study of modern people's reactions to limits of economic growth and to population growth under diverse conditions. It includes a bibliography (pp. 241-277).

A97. Tobin, Sheldon S. "The Future Elderly: Needs and Services." *Aging*. 279-280 (January-February 1978): 22-26.

Congregate services and health needs of the elderly in the future.

MIDDLE AGE

A98. Merriam, Sharan. "Middle Age: A Review of the Literature and Its Implications for Educational Intervention." *Adult
Education* 29(1978):39-54.

The literature of middle age is reviewed within the framework
of the following questions: When is middle age? What are the
psychosocial dynamics of middle age? Is there a midlife crisis?
The article includes extensive references.

A99. Neugarten, Bernice L., ed. *Middle Age and Aging: A
Reader in Social Psychology.* Chicago: University of Chicago
Press, 1968. 596 pp.

Selections emphasize problems of social and psychological
adaptations required as individuals move through the second
half of their lives. Priority has been given to empirical studies
illustrating a relatively wide range of research methods.

A100. Stevenson, Joanne Sabol. *Issues and Crises During
Middlescence.* New York: Appleton-Century-Crofts, 1977. x,
230pp.

This textbook on middle age presents research results in a
manner that nonresearchers can understand.

Bibliography

A101. Entine, Alan D., Jean E. Mueller, and Barbara Beth
Wolin, comps. *Perspectives on Mid-Life: A Selected Bibliography*
Technical Bibliographies on Aging. Los Angeles: Ethel Percy
Andrus Gerontology Center, University of Southern Califor-
nia, 1977. 25pp.

A bibliography, arranged under broad subjects, selected to
bring together knowledge from various disciplines and apply
it to some key midlife issues.

WOMEN

A102. Michigan University. Ann Arbor. Conference on Aging, 26th, Sept. 10-12, 1973. *No Longer Young: The Older Woman in America: Proceedings of the 26th Annual Conference on Aging,* intro. Natalie P. Trager. Occasional Papers in Gerontology, No. 11. Ann Arbor: Institute of Gerontology, University Michigan-Wayne State University, 1975. 120pp.

Papers from a conference on the challenges to women during their life span, discussing problems of present status of older women, projections of future status, mechanisms for change, and resources for change.

Bibliography

A103. Hollenshead, Carol, Carol Katz, and Berit Ingersoll. *Past Sixty: The Older Woman in Print and Film.* Ann Arbor: University of Michigan-Wayne State University Institute of Gerontology, 1977. 52pp.

A bibliography of 289 selected books, journal articles, pamphlets, and films which focus on the woman over sixty.

A104. National Organization for Women. Task Force on Older Women. *Age is Becoming: An Annotated Bibliography on Women and Aging.* San Francisco: Glide Publications, 1976. 36pp.

A selective, annotated bibliography of current literature on the impact of aging on women.

Directories

A105. Shields, Laurie. *Displaced Homemakers: Organizing for a New Life.* New York: McGraw-Hill, 1981. xiv, 272pp.

A description and history of the Alliance for Displaced

Homemakers and a discussion of the problems faced by older women who have lost many of their social and economic roles. There is a directory, by state, of centers, programs, and projects providing services to displaced homemakers.

Statistics

A106. Peace, Sheila M. *An International Perspective on the Status of Older Women.* Washington, D.C.: International Federation on Ageing, 1981. viii, 92pp.

Text, statistics and extensive bibliographies on international aspects of roles and images, demographics, family-related roles, health, and income of older women.

WIDOWS

A107. Lopata, Helena Znaniecka. *Women as Widows: Support Systems.* New York: Elsevier, 1979. 485pp.

Based on a study of over one thousand Chicago area widows, this study provides a descriptive and theoretical study on widowhood, focusing on the societal, community, and personal resources available to each widow and on how these resources are utilized to build economic, service, social, and emotional support systems. The book includes a survey questionnaire (pp. 391-463) and a bibliography (pp. 465-477).

Guides, Handbooks, and Manuals

A108. Fisher, Ida, and Byron Lane. *The Widow's Guide to Life: How to Adjust/How to Grow.* Englewood Cliffs, N.J.: Prentice-Hall, 1981. xv, 207pp.

A resource book for widows to help them handle their personal affairs, provide support through the transition from married woman to widow, and how to establish an identity as a single woman.

A109. Nye, Miriam Baker. *But I Never Thought He'd Die: Practical Help for Widows.* Philadelphia: Westminster Press, 1978. 150pp.

A guide for widows to facing fact, understanding feelings, identifying and carrying out developmental tasks and setting new goals.

Bibliography

A110. Strugnell, Cecile. *Adjustment to Widowhood and Some Related Problems: A Selective and Annotated Bibliography.* New York: Health Sciences Publishing Corp., 1974. 201pp.

An annotated bibliography on all aspects of widowhood, with citations grouped under the general headings Bereavement, Problems Related to Widowhood, Helping Relationships, and Related Bibliographies. One subsection is specifically on the elderly widow.

FAMILY

A111. Kirschner, Charlotte. "The Aging Family in Crisis: A Problem in Living." *Social Casework.* 60(1979):209-216

A study, using case histories, of situations in which the transition to old age becomes a problem for the aged parent and to the adult children.

A112. Troll, Lillian E., Sheila J. Miller, and Robert C. Atchley. *Families in Later Life.* Belmont, Calif.: Wadsworth, 1979. viii, 168pp.

To complement the textbooks that focus on family events in early life, this study deals with the family lives of older people, including those who have never married or never become parents. A bibliography appears on 136-163.

Guides, Handbooks, and Manuals

A113. American Jewish Committee. Institute of Human Relations. *The Aging Parent: A Guide for Program Planners.* New York: 1980. 48pp.

A guide for program planners who disseminate information on resources available to adult children and their aging parents and publicize the enormous problems involved.

A114. Anderson, Margaret J. *Your Aging Parents: When and How to Help.* St. Louis, Mo.: Concordia Publishing House, 1979. 126pp.

Statement of problems met by adult children of aging parents and possible solutions. "Where to Go for Help" appears on pages 113-120.

A115. Gillies, John. *A Guide to Caring for and Coping with Aging Parents.* Nashville, Tenn.: Thomas Nelson, Publishers, 1981. 208pp.

A guide to the care of the frail elderly, both in institutions and in the home. Each chapter is followed by a list of references.

A116. Lauter, Leah, and Elaine B. Jacks. *A Sponsor:s "How To" Guide for Organizing Conferences and Group Seminars on "You and Your Aging Parents."* Garden City, N.Y.: Adelphi University Press, 1978. 32pp.

A manual for setting up conferences or seminars for children of aging parents, or others involved with the care of older people, through a natural support system.

A117. Otten, Jane, and Florence D. Shelley. *When Your Parents Grow Old: Information and Resources to Help the Adult Son or Daughter Cope with the Problems of Aging Parents.* New York: Funk & Wagnalls, 1976. 298pp.

A discussion of the problems of the elderly and solutions available for their children.

A118. Schwartz, Arthur N. *Survival Handbook for Children of Aging Parents.* Chicago: Follett, 1977. 160pp.

A book to help middle-aged children develop an honest dialogue with their older parents in the hope that they can approach their aging parents openly.

A119. Silverstone, Barbara, and Helen Kandel Hyman. *You and Your Aging Parent: The Modern Family's Guide to Emotional, Physical, and Financial Problems.* New York: Pantheon, 1977. 336pp.

A guide for middle-aged children to understanding the problems of aged parents and the actions that may be taken to alleviate these problems.

Bibliography

A120. National Council on the Aging. Library. *Parent-Child Relationships.* Demand Bibliography, new series, no. 1. Washington, D.C.: 1981. [np]

An alphabetically arranged bibliography taken from the card catalog of the NCOA library.

Sex

A121. Butler, Robern N., and Myrna I. Lewis. *Sex After Sixty: A Guide for Men and Women for Their Later Years.* New York: Harper and Row, 1976. 165pp.

A guide to the physical and psychological aspects of sex in older people.

Bibliography

A122. Birren, James E., and Julie L. Moore, eds. Technical Bibliographies on Aging. *Sexuality and Aging: A Selected Bibliography.* Los Angeles: Ethel Percy Andrus Gerontology Center, University of Southern California, 1975. 27pp.

A selected bibliography of references taken from a keysort file of over 45,000 references compiled from commercially available data bases and published sources relevant to gerontology. Entries are arranged alphabetically under broad subject classification.

A123. National Council on the Aging. Library. *Sex.* Demand Bibliography no. 24. Washington, D.C.: 1976. [np].

An alphabetically arranged bibliography on aging and sexual activity taken from the card catalog of the NCOA library.

DEATH

A124. Miller, Marv. *Suicide After Sixty: The Final Alternative.* Springer Series on Death and Suicide, Vol. 2. New York: Springer Publishing Company, 1979. 118pp.

A review of the literature of geriatric suicide and a discussion of the multiple reasons leading to the suicide decision. It contains a bibliography (pp. 106-116).

A125. Schulz, Richard. *The Psychology of Death, Dying, and Bereavement.* Reading, Mass.: Addison-Wesley, 1978. 197pp.

A comprehensive review and critical analysis of the most current literature and research data available on death, dying, and bereavement. It contains a bibliography (pp. 172-187).

A126. Wilcox, Sandra Galdieri, and Marilyn Sutton. *Understanding Death and Dying: An Interdisciplinary Approach.* 2d ed. Sherman Oaks, Calif.: Alfred Publishing Co., Inc., 1981. xiv, 400pp.

A textbook, for use with adult groups, which covers all aspect of death, dying, terminal care, and grief. Each chapter contains an essay by the authors, an encounter, readings from various authors, questions and projects, structured exercises, and a reading list.

Guides, Handbooks, and Manuals

A127. Doyle, Polly. *Grief Counseling and Sudden Death: A Manual and Guide.* Springfield, Ill.: Charles C. Thomas, 1980. xvi, 332pp.

Material basic on a broad understanding of the essential information available on grief and bereavement; how to select people to do grief work, how to train them and how to counsel the bereaved. There are examples of forms to be used. Contains bibliography (pp. 275-321).

A128. Schoenberg, B. Mark, ed. *Bereavement Counseling: A Multidisciplinary Handbook.* Westport, Conn.: Greenwood Press, 1980. xii, 266pp.

A comprehensive, multidisciplinary handbook to guide counselors dealing with bereaved persons.

A129. Ulin, Richard O. *Death and Dying Education.* Washington, D.C.: National Education Association, 1977. 72pp.

A guide for classroom teachers to the design of courses on death and aging. A bibliography lists general works, literary materials, and audiovisual resources.

Bibliography

A130. National Council on the Aging. Library. *Death and Dying.* Demand Bibliography no. 21. Washington, D.C.: 1975. [np]

An alphabetically arranged bibliography taken from the card catalog of the NCOA library, on death and dying.

A131. Oberg, Larry R. "Death and Dying: A Guide to Bibliographical Resources." *Behavioral and Social Sciences Librarian.* 1(Summer 1980):249-262.

A bibliography of recommended readings and bibliographic

sources, including printed bibliographies, indexes and abstracts, journals, nonprint resources, reference works, and statistics.

A132. Sell, Irene L. *Dying and Death: An Annotated Bibliography.* New York: Tiresias Press, 1977. 144pp.

An annotated bibliography which includes 382 journal articles, 71 books, 53 audiovisual citations, author and subject indexes. Material was selected for its relevance to and implications for nursing practitioners, educators, and students involved with providing care for dying patients.

A133. Simpson, Michael A. *Dying, Death, and Grief.* New York: Plenum Press, 1979. xi, 288pp.

A bibliography with evaluative annotations of over 750 books and 200 films and other audiovisual materials. Books are rated by a star system from "strongly recommended" to "not suitable for use at all."

A134. Wass, Hannelore, et al. *Death Education: An Annotated Resource Guide.* Washington, D.C.: Hemisphere Publishing Corp., 1980, xi, 303pp.

A comprehensive guide to the diverse resources currently available in death education, including an annotated bibliography of 384 journal articles and books, 28 detailed descriptions and evaluations of selected textbooks and reference sources, 147 bibliographies, 28 journals and newsletters, 67 references to death attitudes, description of 588 audiovisual resources and 99 organizations, with a summary of suggested community resources.

MINORITIES

A135. Gelfand, Donald E., and Alfred J. Kutzik, eds. *Ethnicity and Aging: Theory, Research, and Policy.* Springer Series on Adulthood and Aging, vol. 5. Springer Publishing Co., 1979. xii, 372pp.

A136. Jackson, Jacquelyne Johnson. *Minorities and Aging.* Belmont, Calif.: Wadsworth Publishing Co., 1980. xiv, 256pp.

An overview of issues pertaining to the study of aging among the minorities of America. Including biological, psychological and social aspects, it deals with life expectancy, support systems, and interaction patterns among elderly minorities and presents models for training professionals to serve this population. A bibliography appears on pages 226-244.

A137. National Council on the Aging. *Employment Prospects of Aged Blacks, Chicanos and Indians.* Washington, D.C.: 1971. 53pp.

Articles that compare the life-styles of the elderly who do not belong to a minority group with elderly poor minority members. Information concerning family living patterns, social and economic conditions, education, social security benefits, health and social services, institutional care, and statistical information is provided.

Bibliography

A138. Balkema, John B. *The Aged in Minority Groups: A Bibliography.* Washington, D.C.: National Council on the Aging. 1973. 19pp.

An annotated bibliography of books and articles on the problems of the minority elderly, arranged by subject.

A139. Ragan, Pauline K., and Mary Simonin, eds. *Black and Mexican American Aging: A Selected Bibliography.* Technical Bibliographies on Aging. Los Angeles: Ethel Percy Andrus Gerontology Center, University of Southern California, 1977. 32pp.

A bibliography of books, articles, dissertations, and papers presented at professional meetings, appearing, with one exception, since 1967.

A140. U.S. Administration on Aging. *The Minority Elderly in*

America: An Annotated Bibliography. DHHS Publication No. (HDS) 80-20071. Washington, D.C.: U.S. Department of Health and Human Services, 1980. 46pp.

An annotated bibliography of 200 items, divided into sections for American Indian, black, Hispanic, Pacific/Asian and cross- cultural, and Asian.

BLACKS

Guides, Handbooks, and Manuals

A141. Dancy, Joseph, Jr. *The Black Elderly: A Guide for Practitioners.* Ann Arbor: The University of Michigan, Wayne State University Institute of Gerontology, 1977. 56pp.

A guide to the needs, problems, and strengths of the black elderly, their cultural heritage and traditions, and attitudes about aging and minorities. It contains a bibliography (pp. 41-55).

Bibliography

A142. Barnes, Nell D. *Black Aging: An Annotated Bibliography.* Public Administration Series: no. 167. Monticello, Ill.: Vance Bibliographies, 1979. 18pp.

An annotated bibliography of books, journal articles, or conference proceedings, and government documents on black aging, primarily from 1970 to 1977.

A143. Davis, Lenwood G. *The Black Aged in the United States: An Annotated Bibliography.* Westport, Conn.: Greenwood Press, 1980. xviii, 200pp.

An annotated bibliography on the black aged, divided into eight sections. There are sections on black aged and slavery, black old folks' homes, and periodicals with articles pertaining to the black aged. The other sections are major books, dissertations and theses, government publications, and articles. Each section is subdivided by subject, but there is no subject index so the citations are not readily accessible by subject. There is an author index.

Statistics

A144. U.S. Congress. Senate. Special Committee on Aging. *The Multiple Hazards of Age and Race: The Situation of Aged Blacks in the United States.* 92d Congress, 1st Session. Washington, D.C.: U.S. Government Printing Office, 1971. 73pp.

Discussion and statistics on population, poverty, residence, income, employment, health, housing and transportation of elderly blacks. A bibliography appears on pages 37-47.

A145. Williams, Blanch S. *Characteristics of the Black Elderly — 1980.* Statistical Reports on Older Americans, No. 5. Washington, D.C.: National Clearinghouse on Aging, 1980. 41pp.

Statistical tables and analyses of marital status, household composition, labor force characteristics, income and poverty, education, health, life expectancy, and mortality.

ASIAN AMERICANS

Statistics

A146. Fujii, Sharon. "Older Asian Americans: Victims of Multiple Jeopardy." *Civil Rights Digest.* 9(Fall 1976):22-29.

Statistical information on elderly Asian Americans.

SPANISH AMERICANS

Bibliography

A147. Delgado, Maria, and Gordon E. Finley. "The Spanish-Speaking Elderly: A Bibliography." *The Gerontologist* 18(1978):387-394.

A classified bibliography containing selected professional, research, and scholarly references regarding the Spanish-speaking elderly from Latin America, Spain, and the United States for the years 1960-1977.

A148. U.S. Human Resources Corporation. *The Spanish-Speaking Elderly: A Bibliography*. San Francisco: The Corporation, 1973. 24pp.

A bibliography on the Spanish-speaking elderly, the elderly in general, and the background on Spanish-speaking communities. Lists books, periodicals, government documents, and other works.

Statistics

A149. Hernandez, Jose, and Lilia Hernandez. *Report on the Senior Citizen Population of Spanish Heritage*. Tucson: Arizona Institute for Research, 1972. 23pp. +appendices.

Population statistics and sources of social and economic statistics for Spanish Americans.

NATIVE AMERICANS

A150. National Indian Conference on Aging, Phoenix, Arizona, June, 1976. *The Indian Elder, A Forgotten American*. Final Report on this first conference, prepared by J. Lyon. Albuquerque, N.M.: Adobe Press, 1978.

This report covers the proceedings of a conference in which 1,500 Native Americans from 171 tribes, including some from

Alaska, participated. The conference investigated the needs of Native Americans and made recommendations for services to meet these needs.

A151. National Indian Council on Aging. *The National Indian Council on Aging: The First Three Years of a National Indian Task Force Operation.* Albuquerque, N.M.: 1980. 161pp.

An overview of the Indians of North America, including problems and solutions and the federal response to unmet needs.

Statistics

A152. U.S. Congress. Senate. Special Committee on Aging. *Advisory Council on the Elderly American Indian: A Statement by Council Members, Together with Analysis of Available Statistical Information and Other Appendixes Material.* Washington, D.C.: U.S. Government Printing Office, 1971. 38pp.

Discussion and statistics on housing, institutional care, nutrition, recreation, transportation, communication, employment, health services, and education of the elderly Native American.

A153. Williams, Blanch S. *American Indian Population, 55 Years of Age and Older: Geographic Distribution, 1970.* Statistical Reports on Older Americans, no. 1. Washington, D.C.: National Clearinghouse on Aging, 1977. 14pp.

Demographic statistics on American Indians age 55 and over taken from the 1970 census.

A154. Williams, Blanch S. *Social, Economic, and Health Characteristics of Older American Indians.* Statistical Reports on Older Americans, no. 4. Washington, D.C.: National Clearinghouse on Aging, 1978. 30pp.

Statistical tables and analyses on marital status, household opposition, labor force characteristics, income and poverty, education, health, life expectancy, and mortality.

RURAL POPULATION

Bibliography

A155. Kim, Paul K.H., and H. Lamprey. *A Bibliography on Rural Aging.* Gerontology Publication Series, 1979-1. Lexington: University of Kentucky, Mental Health and Rural Gerontology Project, 1979.

An annotated bibliography of 553 citations covering the literature of the rural aged through 1978 with a few 1979 references. The entries are in no order, but a code number for each indicates subjects. There is an author index.

A156. Wilkinson, Carroll Wetzel. *Rural Aged in America, 1975-1978: An Annotated Bibliography.* Occasional Papers on the Rural Aged, No. 1. Morgantown: West Virginia University Gerontology Center, 1978. 66pp.

A bibliography of 167 publications on the rural elderly, arranged by author and by subject, followed by an inventory of both past and present research projects on the rural aged.

PSYCHOLOGICAL ASPECTS

Bibliography

A157. Schwartz, Arthur N., ed. *Psychological Adjustment to Aging: A Selected Bibliography.* Technical Bibliographies on Aging. Los Angeles: Ethel Percy Andrus Gerontology Center, University of Southern California, 1975. 68pp.

A selected bibliography of references taken from a keysort file of over 45,000 references compiled from commercially available data bases and published sources relevant to gerontology. Entries are arranged alphabetically under broad subject classification.

SOCIOLOGICAL ASPECTS

A158. Estes, Carroll L., et al. *The Aging Enterprise.* San Francisco: Jossey-Bass, 1979, xiv, 283pp.

A critical examination of social policies and services for the aging. It contains a bibliography (pp. 248-267).

A159. Rosow, Irving. *Socialization to Old Age.* Berkeley: University of California Press, 1975. 188pp.

The major variables of socialization are closely examined, showing that the elderly are subject to negligible socializing forces. Conditions are put forth that should be conducive to the development of roles and norms to which old people could be socialized. A bibliography appears on pages 173 through 188.

A160. Rossi, Robert J., and Kevin J. Gilmartin. *The Handbook of Social Indicators: Sources, Characteristics, and Analyses.* New York: Garland STPM Press, 1980. xvi, 199pp.

A textbook that provides a conceptual grasp of the idea of social indicators and a set of practical guidelines for practitioners of the art. A glossary and bibliography are appended.

Guides, Handbooks, and Manuals

A161. Jacobs, Bella, Pat Lindsley, and Mimi Feil. *A Guide to Intergenerational Programming.* Washington, D.C.: National Council on the Aging, National Institute of Senior Centers, 1976. 28pp.

Suggestions for programs in which old and young are brought together. The first section describes programs, and the second section is a step-by-step guide for implementing a program, and the third section provides a training outline for volunteers or staff.

Bibliography

A162. Bengston, Vern L., Kim Edwards, and Gary A. Baffa. *Intergenerational Relations and Aging: A Selected Bibliography.* Technical Bibliographies on Aging. Los Angeles: Ethel Percy Andrus Gerontology Center, University of Southern California, 1975. 41pp.

A selected bibliography of references taken from a keysort file of over 45,000 references compiled from commercially available data bases and published sources relevant to gerontology. Entries are arranged alphabetically under broad subject classification.

A163. Sharma, Prakash C. *A Selected Bibliographic Research Guide to Attitude Toward Aging.* Public Administration Series no. P 214. Monticello, Ill.: Vance Bibliographies, 1979. 6pp.

Over sixty references to books and journal articles, primarily from the period 1950-1975, related to attitudes toward aging.

A164. Sharma, Prakash C. *Sociology of Retirement: A Selected Bibliographic Research Guide (1950-1973).* Public Adminstration Series no. P 67. Monticello, Ill.: Vance Bibliograpies, 1978. 13pp.

Over 150 references, from the book and journal literature, to studies on the sociology of retirement.

A165. Weiss, Joseph E. *A Bibliography on Migration with Special Emphasis on Sunbelt Migration.* Public Administration Series no. 371. Monticello, Ill.: Vance Bibliographies, 1979. 23pp.

A bibliography of materials on the political, social, and economic effects of migration. The citations were gathered primarily from the 1970–1978 issues of major indexing and abstracting services and selected information banks.

CRIME

A166. Block, Marilyn R. and Jan D. Sinnott. *The Battered Elder Syndrome: An Exploratory Study.* College Park: Center on Aging, University of Maryland, 1979. vii, 133pp.

A study on violence in American society, forms of family violence, elder abuse, methodology, and results of the study, policy conclusions, and a proposed mandatory elder abuse reporting law. A bibliography appears on pages 109-124.

Guides, Handbooks, and Manuals

A167. Edgerton, Julie. *Crime Prevention Handbook for Senior Citizens.* Kansas City, Mo.: Midwest Research Institute, 1977. 53pp.

A handbook describing how one becomes a victim of crime and what practical things can be done to prevent victimization by burglary, robbery, larceny, or fraud.

A168. Goodell, Rita Nitzberg. *Effective Responses to the Crime Problem of Older Americans: An Instructor's Guide.* Washington, D.C.: The National Council of Senior Citizens, Legal Research and Services for the Elderly Criminal Justice and the Elderly Program, 1982.

A course of instruction, with complete lesson plans and supplementary material to be used with the *Handbook,* for 30 classroom sessions of 90 minutes each. "Instructor Guidelines" tell the instructor exactly what to do during each step of each lesson.

A169. Jaycox, Victoria H., Lawrence J. Center, and Edward F. Ansello. *Effective Responses to the Crime Problem of Older Americans: A Handbook.* Washington, D.C.: The National Council of Senior Citizens, Legal Research and Services for

the Elderly Criminal Justice and the Elderly Program, 1982.
278pp.

Basic information on crime problems affecting elders and
countermeasures which have proven most successful.

Bibliography

A170. Boston, Guy. *Crime Against the Elderly: A Selected Bibliography.* Washington, D.C.: U.S. Department of Justice.
National Institute of Law Enforcement and Criminal Justice,
1977. vii, 81pp.

An annotated bibliography of books, journal articles, pamphlets, and audiovisual material on crime against the elderly.
The citations are listed under broad subject categories and the
source of each document is given in an appendix.

A171. Boston, Guy, Rita Nitzberg, and Marjorie Kravitz,
comps. *Criminal Justice and the Elderly: A Selected Bibliography.*
Washington, D.C.: Department of Justice. National Institute
of Law Enforcement and Criminal Justice, 1979. ix, 104pp.

A bibliography, in seven sections, of books, journal articles,
government documents, and unpublished papers and man-
uscripts on crime against the elderly and consumer fraud. All
citations are abstracted and the source for obtaining each
document is given.

A172. Martin, Carol Ann. *The Elderly and Crime—A Dishear-
tening Dilemma: A Selected Bibliography.* Public Administration
Series no. 489. Monticello, Ill.: Vance Bibliographies, 1980.

A bibliography of books, reports, papers, journal articles,
audiovisual materials, and audiocassettes on the topic of
crime and the elderly.

A173. Ormiston, Patricia L. *Violent Crime and the Elderly: A
Bibliography.* Public Administration Series: Bibliography no.
P-762. Monticello, Ill.: Vance Bibliographies, 1981. 19pp.

A bibliography of books, essays, periodical and newspaper articles, dissertations, and government documents printed between 1976 and 1981.

Directories

A174. Gross, Philip J. *Crime Prevention Programs for Senior Citizens.* Gaithersburg, Md.: International Association of Chiefs of Police, 1976. unpaged.

Directory of crime prevention programs arranged by city. Each entry gives name of agency, address, phone number, contact person, name of program, length of operation, annual cost, objectives, activities, benefits, participating agencies, and publications.

POLITICAL ASPECTS

A175. U.S. Congress. Senate. Special Committee on Aging. *Survey of Delegates to the 1981 White House Conference on Aging: A Preliminary Report.* Prepared by the Special Committee and National Retired Teachers Association/American Association of Retired Persons. Washington, D.C. [NRTA/AARP], 1982. 32pp.

Results of a survey of delegates to the 1981 White House Conference on Aging giving the top ten recommendations, the top three priorities for each of the 14 committees, and a discussion of the major themes as reflected in the priority recommendations.

Guides, Handbooks, and Manuals

A176. Hess, Clinton W., and Paul A. Kerschner. *The Silver Lobby: A Guide to Advocacy for Older Persons.* Los Angeles: Ethel Percy Andrus Gerontology Center, University of Southern California, 1978. 45pp.

A blueprint for organizing advocacy efforts for older people.

There are many training exercises and problem-solving cases. Procedures for bringing an unorganized group of older persons into a unified, driving force for change are described.

A177. Kleyman, Paul. *Senior Power: Growing Old Rebelliously.* San Francisco: Glide Publications, 1974. 177pp.

A guideline for political action for the elderly based on the experience of the California Legislative Council for Older Americans.

History

A178. Vinyard, Dale. *Rediscovery of the Aged: "Senior Power" and Public Policy.* Prepared for delivery at the 1976 annual meeting of the American Political Science Association, The Palmer House, Chicago, September 2-5, 1976. 38+7pp. typescript.

A brief history of the politics of the aged and a discussion of agencies and programs for the aged. Extensive bibliography.

LEGAL ASPECTS

A179. U.S. Congress. Senate. Special Committee on Aging. *Developments in Aging, 1959-.* Washington, D.C.: U.S. Government Printing Office, 1963-.

The annual report of the committee which describes actions of the Congress, the administration and the committee that has to do with elders. It also summarizes the federal policies and programs of importance to older people. There are many statistical charts and tables throughout.

A180. U.S. Federal Council on the Aging. *Public Policy and the Frail Elderly.* Washington, D.C.: U.S. Government Printing Office, 1979.

Recommendations for action, principles on which the recommendations are based, and background on both the process of development within the council and recommendations. Actions by other organizations relevant to public policy and the rail elderly are discussed.

A181. U.S. Laws, Statutes, etc. *An Act to Provide Assistance in the Development of New or Improved Programs to Help Older Persons Through Grants to the States for Community Planning and Services and For Training . . . And to Establish . . . An Operating Agency to be Designated as the Administration on Aging.* Public Law 89-73, 89th Cong., H.R. 3708, July 14, 1965. Washington, D.C.: U.S. Government Printing Office, 1965. 8pp.

This is the original Older Americans Act.

Guides, Handbooks, and Manuals

A182. Brown, Robert N., et al. *Rights of Older Persons: The Basic ACLU Guide to an Older Person's Rights.* An American Civil Liberties Union Handbook. New York: Avon Books, 1979. xii, 434pp.

A guide setting forth the rights of older persons under present law and suggestions on how these rights can be protected.

A183. Eglit, Howard C. *Age Discrimination.* 2 vols. Colorado Springs, Colo.: Shepard's/McGraw-Hill, 1982.

A comprehensive guide bringing together the relevant statutory, regulatory, and judge-made law concerning age discrimination.

A184. Narey, Sally B. *Senior Citizens and the Law: To Make You Aware of Your Rights and Potential.* Minneapolis, Minn.: Arthur, Chapman and Michaelson, P.A. and F and M Savings Bank of Minneapolis, 1980. viii, 143pp.

A guide for elders to the federal and state laws and agencies designed to protect their rights.

Bibliography

A185. Murbarak, Jill, Diane Sapienza, and Robert Shimane. "Gerontology and the Law: A Selected Bibliography." *Law Library Journal* 73(Spring 1980):255-335.

A bibliography of articles, bibliographies, books, proceedings and documents on the business, legal, medical, and social science aspects of gerontology.

Directories

A186. American Bar Association. Young Lawyers Division. *The Law and Aging Resource Guide.* Compiled by the Committee on Delivery of Legal Services to the Elderly, with the cooperation of the Commission on Legal Problems of the Elderly. Washington, D.C.: 1981. unpaged. loose-leaf.

A directory of available resources and on-going programs for enhancing legal and advocacy efforts for older persons. Under state, names, addresses, and telephone numbers are given for legal services developer and state ombudsman; legal services; law school courses and clinicals; bar committees and projects; pro bono; state legislative committees; ombudsman programs, and major elderly organizations. There are plans to update the *Guide* periodically.

A187. National Senior Citizens Law Center. *Directory of Legal Services Programs for the Elderly.* Washington, D.C.: 1978. 96pp.

A directory giving regional offices on aging, state offices on aging, legal services programs for the elderly (by state), and legal services developers. Each entry gives name, address, contact person, telephone number, and source of funding.

PROTECTIVE SERVICES

A188. U.S. Congress. Senate. Special Committee on Aging. *Protective Services for the Elderly: A Working Paper,* prep. by

John J. Regan and Georgia Springer. Washington, D.C.: U.S. Government Printing Office, 1977. 129pp.

A report designed to bridge the gap between practice relating to protective services and the law. The appendices give five model statutes to guide states in reforming laws relating to protective services.

Guides, Handbooks, and Manuals

A189. Eisenberg, David M. *Guide for Developing Protective Services for Older Adults*. Philadelphia: Philadelphia Geriatric Center, 1978. iv, 32pp.

A guide to aid area agencies on aging, other social agencies, and persons in the development of protective service programs in their communities.

A190. U.S. Social and Rehabilitation Service. *Report of the National Protective Service Project for Older Adults*. Washington, D.C.: U.S. Department of Health, Education and Welfare, 1971. 153pp.

The report of two demonstration projects, and guidelines for state and local governments for initiation of protective services for older adults.

Bibliography

A191. National Council on the Aging. Library. *Protective Services*. Demand Bibliography no. 29. Washington, D.C.: 1977. [np]

An alphabetically arranged bibliography, taken from the card catalog of the NCOA library, on protective services.

LITERATURE

Bibliography

A192. Kellam, Constance E. *A Literary Bibliography on Aging.*
New York: Council on Social Work Education, 1968. viii,
49pp.

An annotated bibliography of literature about aging, listing
materials under novels, short stories, autobiography and
biography, plays, poetry, essays, and miscellaneous.

A193. Moss, Walter G., ed. *Humanistic Perspectives on Aging:
An Annotated Bibliography and Essay.* Ann Arbor: Institute of
Gerontology, University of Michigan- Wayne State Univer-
sity, 1976. 76pp.

Bibliographies about aging classified under nonfiction,
autobiographies by older authors, drama, essays, novels,
poetry, short stories, and death. A list of films is appended.

COMMUNITY ORGANIZATION AND SERVICES

COMMUNITY
ORGANIZATION
AND SERVICES

Contents

COMMUNITY ORGANIZATION AND SERVICES—GENERAL

B1. Gelfand, Donald E., and Jody K. Olsen. *The Aging Network: Programs and Services.* Springer Series on Adulthood and Aging, no. 8. New York: Springer Publishing Co., 1980. xi, 340pp.

A systematic overview of the breadth and scope of programs and services now available to elderly Americans.

B2. Holmes, Monica Bychowski, and Douglas Holmes, eds. *Handbook of Human Services for Older Persons.* New York: Human Sciences Press, 1979. 300pp.

An overview of eight services that enhance the quality of life and are often alternatives to institutional care. The importance of each service is discussed, as are the public and private agencies and legislation pertinent to the service, service components, and models for delivery. There is an annotated bibliography for each.

B3. Schulberg, Herbert C., Frank Baker, and Sheldon Roen, eds. *Developments in Human Services.* Vol. 1. New York: Behavioral Publications, 1973. 536pp.

Four monographs bound together to form a textbook in service delivery programs and research.

Periodicals

B4. *Aging Services News* (Formerly: *Supportive Services*). 1977. 22/yr. Care Reports, Inc., 4865 Cordell Ave, Bethesda, MD. 20014.

A Washington-based news service, broadly in the fields of

health, housing, and supportive services, that gives current updates on legislation, federal regulations, and congressional and federal problems affecting elders. It highlights funding sources as they become available.

B5. *Journal of Gerontological Social Work.* 1978. q. The Haworth Press, 149 Fifth Ave, New York, NY 10010.

Substantive articles on social work theory and practice in the field of aging, oriented toward the needs of social work administrators, practitioners, and supervisors of long-term care facilities, mental health centers, family service agencies, acute-treatment and psychiatric hospitals, community and senior centers, planning agencies, and public health and welfare agencies.

B6. *Perspective on Aging.* 1972. bi-m. National Council on the Aging, Inc., 600 Maryland Ave, SW, West Wing 100, Washington, DC 10024.

Published for and distributed to members of the National Council on the Aging, this journal contains articles, many of them descriptive of programs, geared to practitioners in the field of aging.

B7. *Senior Center Report* (Formerly: *Memo*). 1971. 10/yr. National Council on the Aging, Inc., 600 Maryland Ave, SW, West Wing 100, Washington, DC 10024.

A newsletter reporting on legislation, regulations, program ideas, and training programs related to elders. It is geared to the interests of senior centers' personnel. Some consumer-related information is included. Information comes from government reports, other newsletters, and contacts with practitioners.

COMMUNITY ORGANIZATION

General Works

Guides, Handbooks, and Manuals

B8. Collins, Marjorie A., and James E. Mills. *Boards and Advisory Councils: A Key to Effective Management.* Washington, D.C.: National Council on the Aging, 1979. 59pp. + appendix.

A handbook for organizations on the creation and functioning of boards and advisory bodies and intra- and inter-organizational functioning. There is a bibliography (pp. A4-A9).

B9. Dunham, Arthur, Charlotte Nusberg, and Sujata Basu Sengupta. *Toward Planning for the Aged in Local Communities: An International Perspective.* Washington, D.C.: International Federation on Ageing, 1978. v, 49pp.

A handbook showing how to create a local planning agency for the aging, suggesting characteristics to help such an agency be effective and listing types of services which may be needed by older persons. A bibliography appears on pages 41-49.

Funding Sources

Directories

B10. Cohen, Lilly, Marie Oppedisano-Reich, and Kathleen Hamilton Gerardi, eds. *Funding in Aging: Public, Private and Voluntary.* 2d ed., rev. and enl. Garden City, N.Y.: Adelphi University Press, 1979. viii, 308pp.

A basic directory of funding agencies giving, for each agency, the program objectives, types of assistance, uses and restrictions, applicant eligibility, beneficiary eligibility application procedures, formula and matching requirements, length and time phasing of assistance, range and average of financial assistance, and information contacts. There is a name and subject index.

B11. Lemaire, Ingrid. *Resource Directory for the Funding and Managing of Nonprofit Organizations.* [New York]: The Edna McConnell Clark Foundation, 1977. 127pp.

A resource directory on where to secure funds, how to secure these funds, and where to secure technical assistance for more effective management.

Programs

B12. Teicher, Morton I., Daniel Thursz, and Joseph L. Vigilante, eds. *Reaching the Aged: Social Services in Forty-four Countries.* Social Service Delivery Systems. An International Annual, Vol. 4. Beverly Hills: Sage Publications, 1979. 256pp.

A series of descriptive and analytic works about programs for the aging in foreign countries, including special program innovations.

Guides, Handbooks, and Manuals

B13. Baumhover, Lorin A., and Joan Dechow Jones, eds. *Handbook of American Aging Programs.* Westport, Conn.: Greenwood Press, 1977. 188pp.

Papers by gerontologists in the areas of planning, direct services, volunteerism, and ombudsmanship.

B14. Hayeland, James. *Grandbook of Programs for the Aging.* West Mystic, Conn.: 1978. viii, 173pp.

Programs that can help elders in local communities and ways to get them started. There are directories of federal, state, and area agencies on aging and a list of national organizations.

B15. United States Conference of Mayors. *Administering Aging Programs.* 5 volumes bound in 1. Washington, D.C.: 1981.

Forms, guides, checklists, information manuals and directories compiled for the use of cities in administering aging programs. The volumes are: 1.*Assessing the Role of Cities in Aging Programs,* 2. *Structuring an Office on Aging,* 3. *Pursuing AAA Designation,* 4. *Mayor's Guide to the OA Act,* 5. *Directory of City Aging Offices.*

B16. Vickery, Florence E. *Creative Programming for Older Adults: A Leadership Training Guide.* New York: Association Press, 1972. 320pp.

A textbook for students preparing to work with elders; a manual of social programs for in-service training of agency staff, aides and technicians; and a guide for leadership training workshops for board, council and committee members, and other volunteers.

B17. Weisman, Celia B. *The Future is Now: A Manual for Older Adult Programs in Jewish Communal Service Agencies.* New York: National Jewish Welfare Board, 1976. 176pp.

A joint project of the Brookdale Foundation and the National Jewish Welfare Board. There are bibliographies throughout the text.

Bibliography

B18. Brown, Ruth E. *Community Action Programs: An Annotated Bibliography.* Council of Planning Librarians. Exchange Bibliography No. 277. Monticello, Ill.: Council of Planning Librarians, 1972. 37pp.

An annotated bibliography of books, journal articles, and reports on the formation and operation of Community Action Agencies.

Directories

B19. Norback, Craig and Peter Norback. *The Older American's Handbook*. New York: Van Nostrand, 1977. 311pp.

A directory listing sources of information and aid for older people under such headings as health, housing, nursing homes, and state agencies on aging.

B20. Schechter, Irma. *Chartbook of Federal Programs in Aging*. Washington, D.C.: Care Reports, Inc., 1980. xvi, 176pp.

A desk reference to federal assistance programs that support aging research, training or services. For each of 164 major programs it gives, under federal agency, program name, purpose, authority, federal unit, funds, eligibility, and perspective on the program. Detailed contents by government department and by function, and miscellaneous information on the departments aid in the use of the book.

B21. U.S. Library of Congress. *Federal Responsibility to the Elderly (Executive Programs and Legislative Jurisdiction)*. Compiled by the Congressional Research Service of the Library of Congress for the Select Committee on Aging, House of Representatives. 95th Congress, 2nd Session. Washington, D.C.: U.S. Government Printing Office, 1979. 16pp.

Charts showing major federal programs benefiting the elderly, by category and agency, employment and volunteer, health care, housing, social service programs, income maintenance, training and research programs and transportation, followed by house and senate committees and subcommittees with jurisdiction over major areas related to the elderly.

Planning

Guides, Handbooks, and Manuals

B22. La Charité, Norman, Rebecca Ryan, and Victor Barocas. *Problems of the Elderly: A Needs Assessment Workbook*.

Bethesda, Md.: Center for Human Services, Research and Development Division, 1981. vi, 165pp.

A step-by-step guide on how to plan and prepare for the collection, analysis and interpretation of information on the problems and needs of the elderly. Bibliography: pp. 163-165.

Bibliography

B23. Ames, David L., and Sharon E. Schulz. *Planning for the Aging: A Selected Bibliography of Planning for the Aging in an Urban and Regional Context.* Vance Bibliographies. Public Administration Series 272. Monticello, Ill.: Vance Bibliographies, 1979. 29pp.

A bibliography of books and journal articles citing primarily the literature of the 1970s on planning and urban studies related to aging. The entries are listed under subject.

National Organizations

Acronyms

B24. Kerschner, Paul A., and Mary F. Power. *Acronyms in Aging.* Washington, D.C.: National Retired Teachers Association/American Association of Retired Persons, 1981. 19pp.

A dictionary of acronyms of organizations concerned with the aging and phrases (e.g., I & R for information and referral) and titles of the Older American's Act and the Social Security Act. A short descriptive paragraph follows each acronym.

Directories

B25. National Association of Social Workers. *Directory of Agencies: U.S. Voluntary, International Voluntary, Intergovernmental.* Washington, D.C.: The Association, 1978. 96pp.

Information on membership, purposes, and programs of more than 300 agencies whose work is related to the profession of social work. The arrangement of entries is alphabetical.

B26. National Council on the Aging. *Directory: National Organizations with Programs in the Field of Aging.* Washington, D.C.: 1971. 95pp.

This directory, arranged alphabetically, includes in each entry, name of organization, address, names of officers, member organizations and affiliates, purpose of organization, its programs and services for the aging, and its publications and audiovisual materials.

B27. Stuebe, Charles, ed. *A Directory of Resources for Aging, Gerontology, and Retirement.* Mankato, Minn.: Scholarly Press, 1979.

A volume containing two directories. The first, of major organizations for aging, gerontology and preretirement, lists, where applicable, the name of the organization, address, executive officer, founding date, membership, and journal publications. It gives an extensive history of each, and describes its activities, services, and research. The second part is a directory of colleges and universities offering degree programs in gerontology. Each entry gives the name and address of the school and the contact person. Courses for older adults are described, as are other courses in gerontology and degree programs. Schools are indexed by type of degree given. There are other indexes of acronyms, organizations, subject, and personal names.

International Organizations

Directories

B28. United Nations. Department of Economic and Social Affairs. *International Directory of Organizations Concerned with the Aging.* New York: United Nations, 1977. viii, 54pp.

This directory of 117 institutions located in Africa, Asia, Europe, Latin America, North America, and Oceania gives name, address, executive officer, nature and aims, organization and personnel, periodicals, and languages for each organization.

Volunteers

B29. Bowles, Elinor. "Older Persons as Providers of Services: Three Federal Programs." *Social Policy* 7(November/December 1976):81-88.

Descriptions of the Foster Grandparents Program, Senior Companion Program and Retired Senior Volunteer Program (RSVP).

Guides, Handbooks, and Manuals

B30. Foley, Louise M., ed. *Stand Close to the Door.* Sacramento, Calif.: California State University School of Social Work, 1976. 135pp.

Papers from a five-day training session that form a handbook for volunteers and outreach workers in programs for the elderly.

B31. Stone, Janet. *Second Careers, Volunteer Program: A Handbook for Creating a Volunteer/Retiree Program.* New York: Mayor's Voluntary Action Center, 1980. 57pp.

A handbook, based on the experiences of the New York City program, outlining the procedures for setting up a volunteer program for retirees.

B32. Western Gerontological Society. *Elders and Voluntarism: Technical Assistance Notebook for Older American Volunteer Programs.* San Francisco: 1981.

A handbook to be used in the development of volunteer programs by and for elders. There is the report of a symposium on senior volunteerism, program profiles, a classified directory of resource people, an annotated bibliography, and a listing of audiovisual resources.

Church Programs

B33. Cook, Thomas C., Jr. *The Religious Sector Explores its Mission in Aging.* Athens, Ga.: National Interfaith Coalition on Aging, 1976. 164 + 84pp.

A report of a survey of programs for the aging under religious auspices. There are an extensive literature review and annotated bibliography.

Guides, Handbooks, and Manuals

B34. Clingan, Donald F. *Aging Persons in the Community of Faith: A Guide for Churches and Synagogues on Ministry with the Aging.* Rev. ed. St. Louis, Mo.: Christian Board of Publication, 1980. xi, 82pp.

A guidebook to assist clergy and lay leaders in organizing and planning an effective ministry for and with elders.

B35. Kerr, Horace L. *How to Minister to Senior Adults in Your Church.* Nashville, Tenn.: Broadman Press, 1980. 139pp.

A step-by-step guide for developing a ministry with elders in a local church. A bibliography is included (pp. 137-139).

B36. McClellan, Robert W. *Claiming a Frontier: Ministry and Older People.* Los Angeles: The Ethel Percy Andrus Gerontology Center, 1977. 126pp.

Covers church programs for the elderly; gives model programs and guidelines for starting programs.

B37. Maves, Paul B. *Older Volunteers in Church and Community: A Manual for Ministry.* Valley Forge, Penn.: Judson Press, 1981. 93pp.

A guide to the recruitment and training of older volunteers for the ministry of the church. Sample forms are reproduced and training sessions are outlined.

B38. Synagogue Council of America. *That the Days May be*

Long in the Good Land: A Guide for Aging Programs for Synagogues. New York: The Council, 1975. 93pp.

Basic "how-to" guidelines for planning, developing, and operating a wide variety of programs and services designed to enhance the quality of life of the elderly.

Bibliography

B39. National Council on the Aging, Inc. Library. *Church Programs.* Demand Bibliography no. 26. Washington, D.C.: 1976. [np]

An alphabetically arranged bibliography taken from the card catalog of the NCOA library, on all aspects of the relations between elders and programs of the church.

Senior Centers

Guides, Handbooks, and Manuals

B40. Jordan, Joe J. *Senior Center Design: An Architect's Discussion of Facility Planning.* Washington, D.C.: National Council on the Aging, 1978. 104pp.

An illustrated guide for architects, building committees, and center administrators planning construction or renovation of Senior Center space. Step-by-step decision-making is carefully examined in the first section of the book; the second covers understanding a Center's physical space needs, design concepts related to aging, and design of building space, systems, and interiors.

B41. Jordan, Joe J. *Senior Centers Facilities: An Architect's Evaluation of Building Design, Equipment and Furnishings.* Washington, D.C.: National Council on the Aging, 1975. 201pp.

These guidelines are based on professional experience and information obtained from nine on-site evaluation surveys of existing centers across the nation.

B42. Leanse, Joyce, Marjorie Tiven, and Thomas B. Robb. *Senior Center Operation: A Guide to Organization and Management.* Washington, D.C.: National Council on the Aging, 1977. xiii, 149pp.

This guide analyzes center initiation, staffing, government, and functioning with community service delivery systems; provides guidelines for planning, evaluation, communication, personnel management, records and record keeping, budgeting, accounting, personnel practices, and training; addresses ways to mobilize resources, use volunteers and consultants, and write proposals. There is an extensive bibliography.

B43. National Council on the Aging. National Institute of Senior Centers. *Senior Center Standards: Guidelines for Practice.* Washington, D.C.: National Council on the Aging, 1978. 64pp.

Designed to be a basic reference tool for developing and operating a senior center, the standards are organized to provide comprehensive guidelines for administrative practices and for program scope and implementation.

B44. Oberlander, DeWayne; Lorraine Lidoff; and Joyce Leanse. *Senior Center Standards: Self-Assessment Workbook.* Washington, D.C.: National Council on the Aging, Inc., 1979. v, 167pp.

A workbook to help senior centers systematically examine and strengthen their operations and programs. It contains a bibliography (pp. 153-157).

B45. Steinfeld, Edward, and Stewart Brecher. *Senior Centers: A Renovation Manual.* Harrisburg, Penn.: Senior Center Institute, 1979. v, 248pp.

This manual was developed to promote more effective use of existing senior center facilities and to provide assistance in the reuse of existing buildings for senior centers. It is profusely illustrated with drawings, designs, and floor plans.

Bibliography

B46. National Council on the Aging. Library. *Senior Centers. Demand Bibliography* no. 35. Washington, D.C.: 1980.

An alphabetically arranged bibliography taken from the card catalog of the NCOA library.

B47. National Council on the Aging. National Institute of Senior Centers. *Selected Bibliography of NCOA Publications Concerning Senior Centers.* Prepared by Publications Review Committee, NCOA Advisory Committee on Centers. Washington, D.C.: 1971. 28pp.

A topical index to all NCOA publications about senior centers to that date. These early publications are seminal to the development of the centers movement.

Directories

B48. National Council on the Aging. National Institute of Senior Centers. *Directory of Senior Centers and Clubs: A National Resource.* Washington, D.C.: NCOA, 1974. 545pp.

A directory of nearly 5,000 centers giving, for each listing, name of program, auspices, date established, staff composition, membership and eligibility, schedule, meal service, and other designated services.

General Works

Guides, Handbooks, and Manuals

B49. The Gerontological Society. *Working with Older People: A Guide to Practice.* Washington, D.C.: U.S. Government Printing Office, 1978. 2 vols. (191 + 207pp.)

A revision of a four-volume series by the same name, published in 1969-1970 by the U.S. Public Health Service, this series is designed to provide basic information to those working with elders as planners, policy makers, and human-service workers. Appendices include a directory of selected organizations involved with aging, an annotated bibliography, and a list of directories.

Bibliography

B50. National Voluntary Organizations for Independent Living for the Aging (NVOILA). *A Selected Annotated Bibliography on Continuum of Services: Long-Term Care for the Elderly.* Washington, D.C.: National Council on the Aging, 1980. 51pp.

A classified bibliography of 73 citations with long annotations or abstracts. Though institutional as well as noninstitutional care is covered, the emphasis is on community care and independent living.

B51. Regnier, Victor, et al. *Mobile Services and the Elderly: A Bibliography.* Council of Planning Librarians. Exchange Bibliography no. 1378. Monticello, Ill.: Council of Planning Librarians, 1977. 21pp.

A bibliography, arranged by broad category, of books, reports, and journal articles on mobile units serving the elderly. Most of the citations are to journal articles, and a large percentage are to papers on health services.

Comprehensive Service Delivery

B52. Carter, Genevieve W., et al., eds. *Case Coordination with the Elderly: The Experiences of Front-Line Practitioners.* Los Angeles: University of Southern California, Andrus Gerontology Center, 1979. 87 + 11pp.

Proceedings and summary findings from a symposium which serve as a textbook for alternative designs for comprehensive service delivery through case service coordination and advocacy.

Guides, Handbooks, and Manuals

B53. Steinberg, Raymond M., and Carter, Genevieve W. *Designing Case Management: A Handbook for Development, Implementation and Evaluation of Case Coordination Programs for the Elderly.* Los Angeles: Ethel Percy Andrus Gerontology Center, University of Southern California, 1982. xii, 230pp.

A handbook presenting the complex subject of case managment with the frail elderly, from the perspective of the planner, administrator, and evaluator.

Bibliography

B54. Steinberg, Raymond M. *Complete Case Coordination Bibliography: Alphabetical and Numerical Listings.* Los Angeles, Andrus Gerontology Center, University of Southern California, 1980.

A catalog of the 994 documents collected as a reference library for a three-year research project on case coordination. The collection includes interim and final reports of case coordination programs, historical documents showing the roots of contemporary case coordination, working papers from research projects, reference volumes, recent conference papers and published journal articles.

Directories

B55. Steinberg, Raymond M., and Valerie C. Jurkiewicz. *A National Directory of Case Coordination Programs for the Elderly, 1979-1980.* Los Angeles. University of Southern California, Andrus Gerontology Center, 1980. unp.

A directory of 330 case-coordinated programs arranged by locality under state listings. Entries give name, address, executive director, telephone number, primary responsibilities, type of community, geographic boundaries, population, and interorganizational linkages. An index brings together similar programs.

Counseling and Casework

B56. Burnside, Irene Mortenson, ed. *Working with the Elderly: Group Process and Techniques.* North Scituate, Mass.: Duxbury Press, 1978. xv, 421pp.

A textbook of group work with the elderly written by a number of authors. At the end of each chapter there are exercises and a bibliography.

B57. Landreth, Garry L., and Robert C. Berg, eds. *Counseling the Elderly: For Professional Helpers Who Work with the Aged.* Springfield, Ill.: Charles C. Thomas, 1980. xxix, 500pp.

An anthology, for counselors, of 51 papers published during the past ten years on the development aspects of aging and the aged.

B58. Lowy, Louis. *Social Work with the Aging: The Challenge and Promise of the Later Years.* Harper Series in Social Work. New York: Harper and Row, 1979. xv, 493pp.

The role of social work practice in working with the aging from the points of view of both history and current developments in policy, practice and demography. Bibliography: pp. 447–461, Organizations: 463–67, Publication and Films: 469 –73, Selected References by Subject: 475–79.

B59. Sinick, Daniel. *Counseling Older Persons: Careers, Retirement, Dying.* New Vistas in Counseling Series, Vol. 4. New York: Human Sciences Press, 1977. 112pp.

Background material on second careers, retirement and dying, followed by counseling emphases in each area. There is an extensive bibliography.

Guides, Handbooks, and Manuals

B60. Ganikos, Mary L. et al. *A Handbook for Conducting Workshops on the Counseling Needs of the Elderly.* Washington, D.C.: American Personnel and Guidance Association, 1979. viii, 47pp.

A handbook to assist counselor educators design a workshop that will help participants identify feelings about their own aging, clarify their attitudes about aging in general, call public and professional attention to the potential counseling needs of older people, and help dispel the common myths and stereotypes about older people. Sample workshop activities are given.

Bibliography

B61. Carter, Beryl, and Sheldon Siegel. *An Annotated Selective Bibliography for Social Work With the Aging.* New York: Council on Social Work Education, 1968. 57pp.

An annotated bibliography covering articles from 1959 to 1967 of interest to social workers, students, and teachers. It includes general reference articles, methodology, settings, programs, and services. Emphasis is on current theories and issues crucial to practice.

Homemaker Services

B62. National Council for Homemaker Services. *Standards for Homemaker-Home Health Aide Services.* New York: 1965. 49pp.

The standards code for homemaker-home health-aide services, including purpose and function, service provision, organization and administration, staffing, orientation and education, records and community responsibility.

B63. _____. *Addenda to Standards for Homemaker-Home Health Aide Services.* New York: 1979. 30pp.

Addenda which supplement and amplify some of the guidelines in the 1965 standards code.

Guides, Handbooks, and Manuals

B64. National Council for Homemaker-Home Health Aide Services. *Widening Horizons: The Teaching Aspect of Homemaker Services—A Guide.* New York, 1974. xi, 113pp.

A guide to the teaching role in homemaker services. Appendixes give a guide for teaching, sample training sessions, national information sources, and recommended reading for homemakers in a teaching role.

B65. *Supplementary Services Guidelines for Services Supplementary to Home Health and Homemaker-Home Health Aide Services.* New York: National Council for Homemaker-Home Health Aide Services, 1977. 32pp.

Discusses meals-on-wheels; friendly visiting; chore, transportation, and escort services; telephone reassurance; and insurance coverage.

Bibliography

B66. Robinson, Nancy, et al. *Costs of Homemaker-Home Health Aide and Alternative Forms of Service: A Survey of the Literature.* New York: National Council for Homemaker-Home Health Aide Services, 1974. 57pp.

The comparison of costs of homemaker-home health aide services to the cost of alternative types of care. There is an extensive annotated bibliography which covers the literature.

Directories

B67. *Directory of Homemaker-Home Health Aide Services.* Approved by the National Council for Homemaker-Home Health Aide Services, Inc. New York: The Council, 1976. 8pp.

Names and addresses of approved agencies are listed

alphabetically by state. The last page lists the basic national standards.

B68. National Council for Homemaker-Home Health Aide Services. *Directory of Homemaker-Home Health Aide Services in the United States, Canada, Puerto Rico and the Virgin Islands.* New York. 1977. 412pp.

A directory, alphabetical by state, of homemaker-home health-aide services. Each entry gives name, address, and telephone number.

Information and Referral

Guides, Handbooks, and Manuals

B69. Tulsa, Oklahoma. City-County Library. *Journal of an Information and Referral Service.* Tulsa: 1977. 33pp.

A basic manual for building and operating an information and referral service in a public library.

Directories

B70. Alliance of Information and Referral Services, Inc. *Directory of Resources.* Reproduction of typescript. Jean Coleman, et al., eds. Phoenix, Ariz.: 1979. Reproduction of typescript.

A listing, alphabetical by state, of AIRS agencies and their publications. The publications include manuals, research studies, reports, handbooks, and thesauri.

ECONOMICS
OF
AGING

ECONOMICS OF AGING

Contents

ECONOMICS—GENERAL

C1. Kreps, Juanita M., et al. *Economics of a Stationary Popula-tion: Implications for Older Americans.* Washington, D.C.: U.S. Government Printing Office, 1977. 91pp.

The ways in which the movement toward zero population growth will affect the ratio of workers to retirees and the impact of these changes in age composition on the productive capacity and the distributive pattern in the economy. A bibliography is included (pp. 83-89).

C2. Schulz, James H. *The Economics of Aging.* 2d ed. Belmont, Calif.: Wadsworth Publishing Co., 1980. xiii, 219pp.

A work to provide noneconomists greater access to the highly technical economics literature dealing with the issues of aging. A bibliography appears on pages 207-219.

Periodicals

C3. *Aging and Work* (Formerly: *Industrial Gerontology*). 1969. q. The National Council on the Aging, Inc., 600 Maryland Ave, SW, West Wing 100, Washington, DC 20024.

The official journal of the National Institute of Aging and Work, formerly the National Institute of Industrial Gerontology. Original articles cover the older worker in relation to job performance, job satisfaction, discrimination, retirement, and other topics in industrial gerontology. Articles are of medium length, carefully documented, readable yet scholarly. There are departments in each issue that give brief news and notes under titles such as ADEA (Age Discrimination in Employment Act), On Capitol Hill, Current Employment Programs, and Mandatory Retirement Issues.

C4. *BNA Pension Reports.* 1976. w. The Bureau of National Affairs, Inc., 1231 25th St, NW, Washington, DC 20037.

Up-to-the-minute news on retirement and employee benefit issues. The report has a summary of contents, a classified index, a section on news, a section on taxes, and a section of text that includes federal regulations and the complete text of articles being reported. There is a concluding "Journal," which is a calendar of meetings, federal and state actions, and events. There are occasional special supplements such as a detailed outline of U.S. Department of Labor compliance documents. The detailed, classified index, which is issued every six weeks with quarterly and semiannual cumulations, is appended by a table of cases, a table of opinions, and a table of regulations and orders.

C5. *Social Security Bulletin.* 1938. m. and *Annual Statistical Supplement.* annual. U.S. Social Security Administration, 6401 Security Blvd, Baltimore, MD 21235.

The official journal of the Social Security Administration. Included are papers with many charts and tables on topics related to work, retirement and social insurance; news from the Social Security Administration; recent legislation; statistical reports, research studies, and extensive tables giving current and retrospective operating statistics.

Each issue of the supplement contains old age, survivors, disability, and health insurance (OASDHI) program definitions; OASDHI historical summary of legislation; supplementary security income (SSI) program definitions; historical summary of SSI legislation; historical summary of aid-to-families-with-dependent-children legislation; and statistical tables on social security and the economy, poverty data, interprogram social security data, OASDHI, SSI, black lung benefits, and public assistance.

Bibliography

C6. Sharma, Prakash C. *Aging and Economy in Modern Society: A Selected Bibliographic Research Guide.* Public Administration

Series: Bibliography no. 199. Monticello, Ill.: Vance Bibliographies, 1979. 12pp.

A bibliography containing nearly 150 selected references on studies, published primarily during 1960 to 1976, pertaining to the economics of aging.

TRANSPORTATION

C7. Applied Resource Integration, Ltd. *Transportation Services: An Examination of Regulatory Problems in Medicaid and Social Service Programs.* Washington, D.C.: 1980. 68pp. + appendices.

The federal statutory, regulatory, and administrative barriers to the use of Title XIX- and Title XX-sponsored programs in the organization and financing of transporation services.

C8. U.S. Administration on Aging. *Transportation for the Elderly: The State of the Art.* DHEW Publication no. OHD 75-20081. Washington, D.C.: U.S. Department of Health, Education and Welfare, Office of Human Development, 1975. 162pp.

Report of a study conducted for AOA by the Institute of Public Administration.

C9. Wachs, Martin. *Transportation for the Elderly: Changing Lifestyles, Changing Needs.* Berkeley, Calif.: University of California Press, 1979. xiv, 262pp.

A methodology for determining the future mobility needs of the elderly as a function of their future locational patterns and travel behavior. Many tables and charts are included, as is a bibliography (pp. 256–262).

Guides, Handbooks, and Manuals

C10. Applied Resource Integration, Ltd. *Implementation Guidelines for Coordinated Agency Transportation Services.*

Washington, D.C.: U.S. Department of Transportation, 1980. 83pp.

Following the *Planning Guidelines* (see citation C11), this is a guide to the development of a system design and financial plan, the signing of agency contracts, and the hiring and training of staff.

C11. Applied Resource Integration, Ltd. *Planning Guidelines for Coordinated Agency Transportation Services.* Washington, D.C.: U.S. Department of Transportation, 1980. 51pp.

The concept of transportation coordination, its potential benefits to the human service agency network and the community, and its applications in a variety of community settings. See also citation C10.

C12. Institute of Public Administration. *Planning Handbook: Transportation Services for the Elderly.* Prepared for the Administration on Aging. Washington, D.C.: U.S. Government Printing Office, 1975. 9 sections separately paged + appendixes.

A manual to be used by area agencies on Aging, State Units on Aging, and others who work with the elderly, as well as by those interested in developing special transportation systems. It outlines all of the steps and procedures for organizing and administering a transportation service for seniors, from planning to the initial opening phase. There are many sample forms, schedule charts, tables, etc.

Bibliography

C13. International Union of Public Transport. *Provisions for Elderly and Handicapped Passengers in Public Transport Systems: Bibliography.* Brussels: 1976. 39pp.

An international bibliography, arranged by country, of books and journal articles on transportation for the elderly and the handicapped. There is an addendum on elderly pedestrians.

C14. Krummes, Daniel C. *Transportation for the Handicapped: An Annotated Bibliography of the Holdings of the Institute of Transportation Studies Library, University of California, Berkeley.* Public Administration Series, Bibliography no. 108. Monticello, Ill.: 1978. 32pp.

A bibliography on transportation for the handicapped, primarily from 1970 to 1978, listed under broad classification. An appendix gives the major indices, abstracts, and catalogs consulted.

C15. Krummes, Daniel C. *Transportation for the Handicapped, Part II: An Annotated Bibliography of Recent Additions to the Holdings of the Institute of Transportation Studies Library, University of California, Berkeley.* Public Administration Series, Bibliography no. 367. Monticello, Ill.: Vance Bibliographies, 1979. 33pp.

This supplement to Krummes's *Transportation for the Handicapped* represents, for the most part, additions to the ITS library collections since July 1978. It is divided into broad subject sections, followed by a geographical index.

C16. Miller, James H., Yupo Chan, and Bennie L. Martin. *A Bibliography on Transporation for Elderly and Handicapped Persons.* Public Administration Series, Bibliography no. P 9. Monticello, Ill.: Vance Bibliographies, 1978. 40pp.

A bibliography of books, journal articles, reports, and speeches arranged alphabetically by title and by subject.

C17. National Council on the Aging, Inc., Library. Demand Bibliography no. 33. *Transportation.* Washington, D.C.: 1980. unp.

An alphabetically arranged bibliography on problems of aging and transportation, taken from the card catalog of the NCOA library.

C18. U.S. Department of Transportation. Transportation Systems Center. *Transportation and the Elderly and Hand-*

icapped: A Literature Capsule. Washington, D.C.: U.S. Government Printing Office, 1977. 83pp.

An introduction to the literature, highlighting the scope of current research and planning in transportation for the elderly and handicapped, selected summaries introducing a wide range of topics, and an annotated bibliography from 1970 to 1977.

EMPLOYMENT

General Works

C19. Jacobson, Beverly. *Young Programs for Older Workers: Case Studies in Progressive Personnel Policies.* Van Nostrand Reinhold/Work in America Institute Series. New York: Van Nostrand Reinhold Co., 1980. vii, 123pp.

A study of personnel policies affecting older employees in the areas of hiring and firing, employing annuitants, flexible work schedules, permanent part-time work, job sharing, job redesign, demotion, retraining, continuing education, educational leaves and sabbaticals, second careers, performance evaluation, salary and pay practices, and benefits.

Guides, Handbooks, and Manuals

C20. Bauer, Dorothy, ed. *Economic Development and the Older Worker: A Technical Assistance Guide for Economic Development Districts.* Washington, D.C.: The National Council on the Aging, Inc., 1979. v, 188pp.

A handbook for economic development district personnel that gives information on economic development and the older worker, data sources, characteristics of middle-aged and older workers, elements of a manpower plan, and a discussion of age discrimination in employment.

C21. Bolles, Richard N. *The Quick Job-Hunting Map.* Berkeley, Calif.: Ten Speed Press, 1979. 37pp.

C22. _____. *What Color is Your Parachute?* Berkeley, Calif.: Ten Speed Press, 1979. 328pp.

The map offers an inventory chart to identify transferable skills and principles for narrowing areas of skill and interest and putting it all together. The book discusses rejection shock, getting help, decisions about job choice, and who has the power for hiring. A resource guide for obtaining further information about job hunting is appended.

C23. Cohen, Leonard. *Choosing to Work.* Reston, Va.: Resont Publishing Company, 1979. 182pp.

Step-by-step techniques, tips, examples, cover letters, and interviews to be used in the job hunt. There is a section to help older workers, the physically handicapped, and minorities overcome employer biases.

C24. Figgins, Ross. *The Job Game: Winning the Job That's Right for You.* Englewood Cliffs, N.J.: Prentice-Hall, 1980. 294pp.

The job search (where and how to look), career and job choice (what you want in a job and what you have to offer), job leads, resume construction, the personal interview, follow-ups, negotiations, and decisions.

C25. Galassi, John P., and Merna Dee Galassi. "Preparing Individuals for Job Interviews: Suggestions from More than 60 Years of Research." *Personnel and Guidance Journal* 57(1968):188-193.

A four-part model to be used in helping prepare individuals for job interviews. There is a list of questions frequently asked during job interviews.

C26. Lembeck, Ruth. *1,001 Job Ideas for Today's Woman: A Checklist Guide to the Job Market.* Garden City, N.Y.: Dolphin Books, Doubleday, 1975. 268pp.

Descriptions of jobs for which the qualifications require little or no training. They range from simple, part-time jobs to professional, full-time jobs. Each job is described, with personal and educational requirements and suggestions for getting started.

C27. National Council on the Aging, Inc. *A Job-Seeking Guide for Seniors.* Prepared by NCOA under a grant from the McDonald's Corporation. Washington, D.C.: 1979. 15pp.

A guide for older job seekers, from resume through the job interview. Public and private sources of help are delineated.

C28. Sprague, Norman, and Hilary Feming Knatz. *Finding a Job: A Resource Book for the Middle-Aged and Retired.* Garden City: Adelphi University Press, 1978. vi, 138pp.

Material on how to look for a job, how to assess skills and interests, how to develop a job search strategy, how to prepare a resume, and how to deal with potential employers.

C29. Winter, Dorothy. *Help Yourself to a Job: A Guide for Retirees.* Boston: Beacon Press, 1976. ix, 158pp.

A discussion of problems in reentering the labor force, public and private sources of help, how to look for work, and suggestions for employers who hire older workers.

Bibliography

C30. McConnell, Stephen R., and Leslie A. Morgan, eds. *The Older Worker: A Selected Bibliography.* Technical Bibliographies on Aging. Los Angeles: Ethel Percy Andrus Gerontology Center, University of Southern California, 1979. iii, 30pp.

A bibliography, arranged by subject, on the older worker and the retirement decision. All works included are published or otherwise available to the public and have been written since 1970.

C31. National Council on the Aging. National Institute of Industrial Gerontology. *Industrial Gerontology: An Annotated Bibliography on Industrial Change and Aging in the Work Force.* New York: The Council, 1968. 32pp.

Research findings relating to aging in the work force. Includes sources of information on the older worker's potentials as a learner and as an employee, references on private pension plans, discrimination in employment, and standard statistical sources of various employment data classified by age groups, education, and other pertinent topics.

Statistics

C32. Chan, Teresita, and Donald G. Fowles. *The Older Worker.* Statistical Reports on Older Americans, no. 6. Washington, D.C.: U.S. Government Printing Office, 1980. 35pp.

Statistical reports and tables on selected characteristics of older workers, such as sex, race, marital status, education, industry, occupation, part-time work, self-employment, unemployment, and desire to work.

Discrimination

C33. Kendig, William L. *Age Discrimination in Employment.* New York: American Management Associations, 1978. 83pp.

The forms of age discrimination in employment and what individuals and organizations can do about it.

C34. Spalding, J.B. "Self-inventory Methods in Preparation for Aged Discrimination Complaints and Lawsuits." *Aging and Work.* 2(1979):246-258.

A method by which employers can reduce their vulnerability to age discrimination complaints and lawsuits, a basis for self-monitoring organizational hiring practices, and a statistical approach to data accumulation and treatment.

Women

Bibliography

C35. Astin, Helen S., Nancy Suniewick, and Susan Dweck. *Women: A Bibliography on Their Education and Careers.* New York: Behavioral Publications, 1974. 243pp.

A bibliography of 352 citations with abstracts. Many of the entries concern the continuing education, second careers, and education of older women.

C36. Elkin, Anna. *The Emerging Role of Mature Women: Basic Background Data in Employment and Continuing Education.* New York: Federation Employment and Guidance Service, 1976. 20pp.

A selected annotated bibliography of free and inexpensive materials.

Job Performance

Bibliography

C37. Kelleher, Carol H., and Daniel A. Quirk. "Age, Physical Capacity and Work: An Annotated Bibliography." *Industrial Gerontology.* 19(Fall 1973):80-98.

An annotated bibliography arranged under the topics: Measurement of Functional Age; Job Analysis Techniques; Evaluating On-the-Job Performance; and Testing, Retraining and Matching Workers to Jobs.

Placement

C38. Anderson, Karen K., and Joanne Fine. "Older Workers and Client-Centered Placement Services." *Aging and Work.* 1(1978):52-57.

Report on a model older worker employment project (RENEW) carried out in five states. Senior aides are trained to work as older worker specialists in local job service employment offices, finding jobs for other older workers.

C39. Rosenberg, Selene M. *How to Start an Employment Service for Senior Citizens.* rev. ed. White Plains, N.Y.: Senior Personnel Employment Council of Westchester, 1978. 13pp. and appendixes. Reproduction of typescript.

A manual, in outline form, for starting a senior employment service.

C40. Wilson, Thurlow R., Deborah H. Bercini, and John A. Richards. *Employment Services for Older Job Seekers.* Alexandria, Va.: Human Resources Research Organization, 1978. xiv, 225pp.

This study of employment services available to older workers analyzes employment assistance and recommends needed improvements. It includes a bibliography (pp. 143-146).

Second Careers

Bibliography

C41. National Council on the Aging, Inc., Library. *Second Careers.* Demand Bibliography no. 34. Washington, D.C.: 1980. unp.

A bibliography, taken from citations in the card catalog of the NCOA library and from entires in *Current Literature on Aging.*

Sheltered Workshops

Bibliography

C42. National Council on the Aging. Library. *Sheltered Workshops.* Demand Bibliography No. 19. Washington, D.C.: 1975. unp.

An alphabetically arranged bibliography on sheltered workshops and the elderly, taken from the card catalog of the NCOA library.

INCOME

General Works

C43. Barnes, John. *More Money for Your Retirement.* New York: Harper and Row, 1978. vi, 307pp.

Money management during retirement years and how to deal with wills, estates, and taxes.

Guides, Handbooks, and Manuals

C44. Rosefsky, Robert. *Rosefsky's Guide to Financial Security for the Mature Family.* Chicago: Follett, 1977. 301pp.

Detailed financial advice for people looking toward retirement and people who have retired.

Statistics

C45. Fowles, Donald G. *Income and Poverty Among the Elderly: 1975.* Statistical Reports on Older Americans, No. 2. Washington, D.C.: National Clearinghouse on Aging, 1977. 13pp. + tables.

A statistical report on the money or cash income and poverty status of older Americans, taken from a March 1976 survey.

C46. U.S. Social Security Administration. Office of Research and Statistics. *Income and Resources of the Aged.* Washington, D.C.: U.S. Government Printing Office, 1980. 35pp.

Statistical charts and graphs on 17 subjects concerned with age and income.

Budgets

C47. U.S. Bureau of Labor Statistics. *Three Budgets for a Retired Couple, Autumn 1980.* Washington, D.C.: 1981.

An annual publication that gives a low-level, intermediate, and high-level budget for a retired couple, made up of hypothetical lists of goods and services that were specified in the mid-1960s to portray three relative levels of living. The tables make adjustments for rural/urban dwelling and for major metropolitan areas throughout the country. The 1981 budget (to be published in late summer 1982) will be the last of this series.

INCOME SOURCES

Bibliography

C48. Coppa and Avery Consultants. *Income Security: A Bibliographic Overview.* Public Administration Series, Bibliography no. P-477. Monticello, Ill.: Vance Bibliographies, 1980. 13pp.

Selected citations in the field of income security, arranged under the headings introductory selections, family assistance plan, income maintenance, employment, old age, pensions, and unemployment insurance.

C49. Employee Benefit Research Institute. *Bibliography of Research: Retirement Income and Capital Accumulation Programs.* 2d ed. Washington, D.C.: 1981. each section paged.

A bibliography summarizing research on the characteristics, costs, and utilization of pension and capital-utilization plans under current and proposed programs. It includes the economic, demographic, and regulatory aspects of providing retirement income. There are sections on completed research, research in progress, and information sources. There are author, title, sponsoring organization, and subject indexes.

C50. Heidbreder, Elizabeth M. *Retirement Income: A Selected Bibliography of Facts, Issues, and Practical Information.* Washington, D.C.: National Council on the Aging, 1972. 10pp.

An annotated bibliography of articles and books, including government publications, pertaining to retirement budgets, private and public pensions, and Social Security.

CONSUMERISM

C51. Schutz, Howard G., Pamela C. Baird, and Glenn R. Hawkes. *Lifestyles and Consumer Behavior of Older Americans.* New York: Praeger, 1979. xvi, 276pp.

Definition of lifestyle patterns existing among older people and relation of lifestyle to consumer behavior in consumer problems, buying style, store choice, income management, health care, food and nutrition, transportation, housing and clothing. A bibliography is included (pp. 264-273).

Directories

C52. Wasserman, Paul, and Jean Morgan, eds. *Consumer Sourcebook*. 2 vols. 2d ed. Detroit: Gale Research Co., 1978.

A comprehensive compilation giving primary information sources available to the consumer. It presents government organizations, voluntary associations, centers, etc.; media services; companies and trade names; a selected bibliography; and indexes to organizations, personnel, and titles. Each entry gives, where appropriate, the name of the organization, the consumer department and the telephone number, the name and title of the person who is the contact for aid with consumer problems.

Statistics

C53. *Guide to Consumer Markets*. New York: The Conference Board, Annual. 295pp.

A series of annual guides giving statistics on population growth and statistics, labor force and employment, consumer income and expenditures, and the prediction, distribution and prices of consumer goods and services. Tables and charts describe current trends in historical perspective and projections into the future.

PENSIONS

C54. American Council of Life Insurance. *Pension Facts*. New York: annual.

The 1980 edition has chapters, including charts and tables, on major pension and retirement programs in the U.S., insured pension plans, private nonlife-insurance company plans, government administered plans, historical growth of pension plans, pension topics of current interest, and the language of pensions, and includes bibliography and the 1974 pension reform law.

C55. Dunetz, Martin R. *How to Finance Your Retirement.* Reston, Va.: Reston Publishing Co., Inc., 1979. xii, 227pp.

Examination of specific types of investments that are particularly applicable to retirement programs. A bibliography is included (pp. 215-221).

Guides

C56. U.S. Labor-Management Services Administration. *Know Your Pension Plan: Your Pension Plan Checklist.* Washington, D.C.: U.S. Government Printing Office, 1979. 16pp.

A series of checklists to guide workers to an understanding of the pension plans under which they are covered.

Bibliography

C57. Walsh, Sandra A. *Bibliography on Public and Private Pension Plans.* Public Administration Series, Bibliography no. 136. Monticello, Ill.: Vance Bibliographies, 1978. 12pp.

A bibliography, divided into book and journal citations and subdivided by country, on pensions.

LIFE INSURANCE

Bibliography

C58. Institute of Life Insurance. *A List of Worthwhile Life and Health Insurance Books.* New York: 1976. 80pp.

An authoritative reference guide to current writings on personal insurance.

Statistics

C59. American Council of Life Insurance. *Life Insurance Fact Book*. Washington, D.C.: annual.

The year's developments in life insurance, described in text, tables, charts, and historical outline.

SOCIAL SECURITY

General Works

C60. Ball, Robert M. *Social Security Today and Tomorrow*. New York: Columbia University Press, 1978. xxiii, 528pp.

The former commissioner of Social Security answers the most frequently asked questions about Social Security and explains the complex provisions of the Social Security law.

C61. Derthick, Martha. *Policymaking for Social Security*. Washington, D.C.: The Brookings Institution, 1979. xiv 446pp.

How Social Security was successfully institutionalized in the four decades after its enactment in 1935, and why it is in trouble today.

C62. Melemed, Brina B. *Title XX of the Social Security Act: A Resource for Serving the Needs of Older People*. Washington, D.C.: National Council on the Aging, 1976. 35pp.

An overview and discussion of Title XX, of the Social Security Act, that was designed to serve as a guide to planning for individuals and groups.

C63. Myers, Robert J. *Social Security*. 2d ed. Bryn Mawr, Penn.: McCahan Foundation, 1981. xxxiv, 925pp.

A factual description of the various social insurance and allied programs now operating in the United States. A bibliography is included (pp. 897-910).

C64. Stein, Bruno. *Social Security and Pensions in Transition: Understanding the American Retirement System*. New York: Free Press, 1980. xx, 308pp.

A clarification of the complex issues of social security and a presentation of a set of alternative policies. Bibliography (pp. 286-297).

C65. Walton, W. Robert. *The Retirement Decision: How the New Social Security and Retirement Age Laws Affect You*. Kansas City, Kans.: Sheed Andrews and McMeel, 1978. 116pp.

How the new Social Security laws affect those already retired and those contemplating retirement.

Guides, Handbooks, and Manuals

C66. Commerce Clearing House, Inc. *Social Security Explained, 1980*. Chicago: 1980. 250pp.

A handbook for those who need a concise explanation of the Social Security program. It includes benefit, replacement rate, historical benefit, and tax tables; a review of the social security system, social security and hospital insurance taxes; coverage, both for employees and the self-employed; and benefits.

C67. National Underwriter Co. *Social Security Manual*. Cincinnati, Ohio: annual.

A manual in eleven sections, using the question-and-answer format to explain in nontechnical terms all facets of Social Security and Medicare benefits. There is a detailed index and an appendix of Social Security tables.

C68. U.S. Social Security Administration. Office of Research and Statistics. *Social Security Programs Throughout the World*. Washington, D.C.: U.S. Government Printing Office, 1938- . Issued biennially since 1938 by the Social Security Administration. Later issues are included in its Research Report Series.

The 1980 revision (Research Report No. 54) gives information on the national Social Security systems of 134 countries, each

displayed on a two-page chart. These charts are divided verti-
cally into dates of basic laws and types of programs; coverage;
source of funds; qualifying conditions; cash disability, and
medical benefits; survivor and dependent benefits; and
administrative organization. They are divided horizontally
into the five major social security branches.

Bibliography

C69. Musgrave, Gerald. *Social Security in the United States: A
Classified Bibliography.* Public Administration Series, Bibliography no. 49. Monticello, Ill.: Vance Bibliographies, 1978.
45pp.

A classified bibliography of books, journal articles, papers,
conference proceedings, and government documents on all
aspects of the Social Security system.

C70. Musgrave, Gerald. *Social Security Worldwide: A Classified
Bibliography.* Public Administration Series, Bibliography no.
P1. Monticello, Ill.: Vance Bibliographies, 1978. 26pp.

An international bibliography, arranged by subject and by
country, of English-language materials on Social Security.

Supplementary Security Income (SSI)

Statistics

C71. Kochhar, Satya. "SSI Recipients in Domiciliary Care
Facilities: Federally Administered Optional Supplementation, March 1976." *Social Security Bulletin.* 40(December
1977):17-28.

Statistics for all states on SSI recipients in homes for the aged
and other domiciliary care facilities.

C72. Rigby, Donald E., and Elsa Ponce. *The Supplemental Security Income Program for the Aged, Blind and Disabled: Selected
Characteristics of State Supplementation Programs as of October
1979.* Social Security Administration Publication no.

13-11975. Washington, D.C.: U.S. Government Printing Office, 1980. v, 103pp.

The third report since 1974 on selected characteristics of state supplementation programs, about which the Social Security Administration most frequently receives inquiries. Summaries are given by state.

RETIREMENT

C73. Harris, Louis, and Associates, Inc. *1979 Study of American Attitudes Toward Pension and Retirement: A Nationwide Survey of Employees, Retirees and Business Leaders.* New York: Johnson and Higgins, 1979. xi, 112pp.

Results of a nationwide survey of 1699 current and retired employees and 212 companies. Particular attention is paid to findings on inflation and the quality of retired life; mandatory retirement; attitudes toward private pensions; and attitudes toward Social Security.

Guides, Handbooks, and Manuals

C74. Biegel, Leonard. *Best Years Catalogue: A Source Book for Older Americans, Solving Problems and Living Fully.* New York: G.P. Putnam's Sons, 1978. 224pp.

A compilation of sources and resources, illustrated and compiled like a catalog, for living for elders.

C75. Finklehor, Dorothy C. *The Triumph of Age: How to Feel Young and Happy in Retirement.* Chicago: Follett, 1979. 264pp.

Guidelines to achieving the attitudes necessary for happiness in retirement, and practical advice for dealing with particular problems. A bibliography appears on pages 261-264.

C76. U.S. Admininistration on Aging. *To Find the Way to Opportunities and Services for Older Americans.* DHEW Publication OHD 75-20807. Washington, D.C.: AoA, 1975. 44pp.

A guide to programs and services available to retirees.

C77. Witkin, Ruth K., and Robert J. Nissen, eds. *How to Live Better After 60: A Guide to Money, Health, and Happniess.* New York: Regency Press, 1978. 280pp.

A retirement guide that discusses the subjects of finances, health, housing, leisure time, legal services, and estate planning. Each subject includes basic information and a manual for self-help.

RETIREMENT AGE

C78. Walker, James W., and Harriet L. Lazer. *The End of Mandatory Retirement: Implications for Management.* New York: John Wiley and Sons, 1978. xv, 223pp.

Management-oriented, this book examines the legal rights of employees and employers, analyzing the effects of the legislation raising the mandatory retirement age. It includes a bibliography (pp. 207-215).

RETIREMENT PLANNING

C79. Adler, Joan. *The Retirement Book: A Complete Early-Planning Guide to Finances, New Activities, and Where to Live.* New York: Morrow, 1975. xiv, 303pp.

Such topics as budgeting, second careers, volunteer work, emotional adjustment, education, living abroad, housing, and health are covered.

C80. Buckley, Joseph C. *The Retirement Handbook.* 6th rev. and enl. ed. by Henry Schmidt. New York: Harper and Row, 1977. xii, 364pp.

A new edition of a handbook, first published in 1953, which gives information on the basic problems of retirement and on retirement careers.

C81. Dickinson, Peter A. *The Complete Retirement Planning Book: Your Guide to Happiness, Health, and Financial Security.* New York: Dutton, 1976. 278pp.

A retirement planning guide which covers health, income, housing, legal needs, and leisure-time activities.

C82. Kinzel, Robert K. *Retirement: Creating Promise out of Threat.* New York: AMACOM, Division of American Management Associations, 1979. 131pp.

A step-by-step guide through the process of creating a retirement plan.

Bibliography

C83. Migliaccio, John N., and Peter C. Cairo. "Preparation for Retirement: A Selective Bibliography, 1974 to 1980." *Aging and Work.* 4(Winter 1981):31-41.

Annotated references to publications identifying important issues in retirement planning and describing retirement programs.

C84. National Council on the Aging Library. *Pre-Retirement Planning.* Demand Bibliography no. 20. Washington, D.C.: 1975. unp.

An alphabetically arranged bibliography on retirement planning, taken from the card catalog of the NCOA library.

HOUSING

HOUSING

Contents

Guides, Handbooks, and Manuals

D1. McConnell, Stephen R., and Carolyn E. Usher. *Intergenerational House-Sharing: A Research Report and Resource Manual.* Los Angeles: Ethel Percy Andrus Gerontology Center, University of Southern California, 1980. viii, 52pp.

An examination of house-sharing agencies and institutional barriers to house-sharing. A resource directory of shared housing projects, a model house-sharing agreement, and a homeowners survey instrument are appended.

D2. Sumichrast, Michael, Ronald Shafer, and Marika Sumichrast. *Where Will You Live Tomorrow? The Complete Guide to Planning for Your Retirement Housing.* Homewood, Ill.: Dow Jones-Irwin, 1981. vii, 313pp.

A guide to major issues of housing costs, designs, planning, and regulations which face retirees and preretirees, based on the suggestions and experiences of more than 1,400 retirees. There are many useful tables and lists, such as "life expectancies of various parts of the house."

Bibliography

D3. Casto, Marilyn Dee, and Savannah S. Day. *Housing for the Elderly—Design, Economics, Legislation and Socio-Psychological Aspects.* Exchange Bibliography no. 1128. Monticello, Ill.: Council of Planning Librarians, 1976. 30pp.

A bibliography pertaining to many aspects of housing the elderly. Included are references from the U.S., England, and Canada from 1956 through 1975. Approximately 375 entries are divided into five major sections: Design and construction, Economic aspects, Legislation, Psychological implications, and General considerations.

D4. Duensing, Edward, and Evelyn L. Klinger. *Age-Segregated Housing: Its Impact on Elderly Americans and Real Estate Markets*. Public Administration Series, Bibliography no. 416. Monticello, Ill.: Vance Bibliographies, 1980. 22pp.

This bibliography draws together the current materials on age-segregated housing and attempts to be complete in all phases of concentrated housing types for the independent elderly.

D5. Garen, Wendy, et al. *Alternatives to Institutionalization: An Annotated Research Bibliography on Housing and Services for the Aged*. Urbana, Ill.: Housing Research and Development, University of Illinois, 1976. v, 137pp.

An annotated research bibliography of books and journal articles on housing and services for the aging. The citations are listed under seven headings, with cross references.

D6. Regnier, Victor A., ed. *Environmental Planning for the Elderly: A Selected Bibliography*. Technical Bibliographies on Aging. Los Angeles: Ethel Percy Andrus Gerontology Center, University of Southern California, 1975. 59pp.

A bibliography of books and journal articles on environment, housing, selected services, and transportation for the elderly.

D7. Rengers, Rosemary. *Design and Social Planning in Housing for the Elderly, 1975-1977: An Annotated Bibliography*. Foreword by Thomas H. Jenkins. Architecture Series, Bibliography no. A13. Monticello, Ill.: Vance Bibliographies, 1978. 140pp.

A bibliography, divided into six topic sections, which lists major sources of information available on design and social planning of housing for the elderly, both from the standpoint of the provider and the consumer. Most citations are annotated. There are appendixes which list directories, national resource groups, and selected periodicals and newsletters.

D8. Sharma, Prakash C. *A Selected Research Guide to Age Segregated Housing for the Elderly Poor.* Public Administration Series, Bibliography no. P100. Monticello, Ill.: Vance Bibliographies, 1978. 9pp.

Nearly 100 citations from the book and journal literature, 1960-1975, on age-segregated housing for the elderly poor.

D9. Sigel, Lois. *Multigenerational Considerations in Planning Environments for the Elderly: An Annotated Bibliography.* Architecture Series, Bibliography no. A 395. Monticello, Ill.: Vance Bibliographies, 1980. 19pp.

An alphabetical, annotated bibliography on the effect of age mixing on elderly persons. A large proportion of the citations are on retirement communities, housing, and living environments.

D10. Sigel, Lois. *Psychosocial Issues Relevant to Creating Environments for the Aging: A Selected Annotated Bibliography, 1955 to the Present.* Architecture Series, Bibliography no. A31. Monticello, Ill.: Vance Bibliographies, 1979. 35pp.

A bibliography with extensive abstracts of books and journal articles on environmental planning in the sense of the development of ambience and not the construction of buildings, per se.

D11. Steidl, Rose E., and Linda M. Nelson. *The Ergonomics of Environmental Design and Activity Management for the Aging.* Exchange Bibliography no. 255. Monticello, Ill.: Council of Planning Librarians, 1972. 76pp.

A review article and a selected annotated bibliography on aging persons' problems of coping with their immediate environment, the implications for environmental design, and activity management.

D12. U.S. Department of Housing and Urban Development. Library Division. *The Built Environment for the Elderly and the Handicapped: A Selective Bibliography*. 2d ed. rev. Washington, D.C.: U.S. Government Printing Office, 1979. 66pp.

A selective, partially annotated, list of monographs and periodical articles issued since 1970, pertaining directly or indirectly to housing and living arrangements for the elderly and the handicapped. Citations are listed under broad subject headings. An author index is appended.

D13. Wellar, Barry S., and Thomas O. Graff. *Introduction and Selected Bibliography on the Quality of Housing and its Environment*. Exchange Bibliography no. 270. Monticello, Ill.: Council of Planning Librarians, 1972. 34pp.

A selected body of references which represent both the methodological and practical aspects of research and development related to housing-environment quality.

Directories

D14. American Association of Homes for the Aging. *Membership Directory*. Washington, D.C.: The Association, 1976. 136pp.

A directory or member homes and facilities arranged alphabetically by state. Each entry gives name, address, phone number, administrators, sponsorship and auspices. There are codes to indicate type of housing, degree of health care, and the kind of outreach services.

D15. Huff, Robert L. *National Directory of Retirement Facilities*. 3 vols. Washington, D.C.: National Retired Teacher's Association/American Association of Retired Persons, 1979.

A catalog, arranged by state, of nonprofit agencies and government-funded housing projects designed and developed for elders. Each entry includes name and address, sponsorship, and facility description.

D16. National Newspaper Publishers Association. *Registry of Private Fair Housing Organization/Groups.* Washington, D.C.: U.S. Department of Housing and Urban Development. Office of Fair Housing and Equal Opportunity.

Provides uniform data about organizations involved in fair-housing activities.

D17. U.S. Department of Housing and Urban Development. Office of Housing. *U.S. Housing Developments for the Elderly or Handicapped.* Prepared by the Office of Multifamily Housing Development. Washington, D.C.: U.S. Government Printing Office, 1979. 119pp.

A listing of all elderly-housing developments funded under Sections 202, 231, and 236 prior to the enactment of the Housing and Community Development Act of 1974.

Statistics

D18. U.S. Department of Housing and Urban Development. *Annual Housing Survey, 1973: Housing Characteristics of Older Americans in the United States.* Washington, D.C.: U.S. Government Printing Office, 1979. viii, 178pp. + appendices.

A detailed statistical analysis of housing of the elderly, prepared from data of the 1973 Annual Housing Survey under the direction of M. Powell Lawton.

ARCHITECTURE AND DESIGN

D19. Goldenberg, Leon. *Housing for the Elderly: New Trends in Europe.* New York: Garland STPM Press, 1981. 199pp.

A profusely illustrated study of housing for the elderly in major European countries. It summarizes the different approaches and lists housing options. There is a directory of organizations concerned with elderly housing and services. A bibliography is included (pp. 189-192).

Guides, Handbooks, and Manuals

D20. Gelwicks, Louis E., and Robert J. Newcomer. *Planning Housing Environments for the Elderly.* Washington, D.C.: National Council on the Aging, 1974. 120pp.

Written for the purpose of improving housing environments for the elderly by acquainting policy makers with the issues. Background information and gerontological theory are translated into step- by-step guidelines for planning and designing a housing project for the elderly.

D21. Thompson, Marie McGuire. *Housing for the Handicapped and Disabled: A Guide for Local Action.* Washington, D.C.: National Association of Housing and Redevelopment Officials, 1977. 176pp.

A guide to assist local groups wishing to build or acquire housing for citizens who are physically handicapped, mentally retarded, or developmentally disabled. Appendixes give sample forms and schedules, and a bibliography is included (pp. 79-83).

Bibliography

D22. Harris, Howard, and Anne Griffiths. *An Annotated Bibliography on the Architectural Design Implications of Residential Homes for Old People.* Architecture Series, Bibliography no. A 45. Monticello, Ill.: Vance Bibliographies, 1979. 80pp.

An alphabetical, annotated bibliography of book and journal literature on architecture and design for retirement communities. Much irrelevant material is included and is so designated.

D23. Koncelik, Joseph A. *Considerate Design and the Aging: Review Article with a Selected and Annotated Bibliography.* Exchange bibliography no. 253. Monticello, Ill.: Council of Planning Librarians, 1972. 12pp.

This review of literature is devoted to recent publications that delineate criteria for designers of products and interiors specifically created for the personal environment of older people. An annotated bibliography appears on pages 7-12.

ARCHITECTURAL BARRIERS

Guides, Handbooks, and Manuals

D24. U.S. Department of Education. *Architectural Barriers Removal: Resource Guides.* Washington, D.C.: U.S. Government Printing Office, 1980. 34pp.

Directories of information resources and funding sources on architectural barriers, an annotated list of publications available from Federal sources, and ordering addresses.

Bibliography

D25. Swanick, M. Lynne Struthers. *Architecture and the Handicapped: A Checklist of Sources.* Architecture Series, Bibliography no. A 279. Monticello, Ill.: Vance Bibliographies, 1980. 8pp.

An international bibliography of journal articles, yearbooks, newspaper items, papers, and government documents on barrier-free architectural design, arranged alphabetically.

D26. U.S. Architectural and Transportation Barriers Compliance Board. *Resource Guide to Literature on Barrier-Free Environments, With Selected Annotations.* Washington, D.C.: U.S. Government Printing Office, 1980. 279pp.

Over 1,400 annotated citations to the literature of barrier-free environments, arranged by subject. Appendices cover travel guides for handicapped travelers, periodicals related to barrier-free environments, and organizations, and there is a subject index.

Directories

D27. National Center for a Barrier Free Environment. *Accessibility Assistance: A Directory of Consultants on Environments for Handicapped People.* Washington, D.C.: U.S. Government Printing Office, 1978. 202pp.

A directory of consultants in three sections. The first section is arranged geographically. Each entry gives name, address, telephone number, professional category, type of services available, and a brief summary of experience, with up to two references. In the second section the consultants are listed alphabetically within categories, and the third section is an alphabetical name index.

FINANCE

Guides, Handbooks, and Manuals

D28. American Association of Homes for the Aging. *Planning and Financing Facilities for the Elderly: A Resource Handbook.* Washington, D.C.: 1978. xi, 281pp.

A variety of financing alternatives for groups concerned with housing, health care, or services for the elderly. Twenty-six illustrated case studies are given as examples. There is a glossary, and appendices give directory information on foundations, organizations, and public and private agencies.

D29. *Housing for the Elderly: A Funding Manual.* Sacramento, Calif.: Area Four Agency on Aging, 1976. 79pp.

Designed to address the questions most frequently asked by agencies and organizations on the availability of funding for housing planning and development.

HOME REPAIR

D30. Campbell, John G. *Home Repair and Handyman Services* *for the Elderly: A Working Paper.* Concord, N.H.: New England Non-Profit Housing Development Corporation, 1977. 17pp.

In addition to available community services, this publication provides information on how to apply for HUD Section 312 Rehabilitation Loans and Farmers Home Administration Section 504 Home Repair Loans and Grants.

CONGREGATE HOUSING

Guides, Handbooks, and Manuals

D31. Hanaway, Lorraine. *The Three-in-One House: A Guide to Organizing and Operating a House for Three Older Persons.* Frederick, Md.: Home Care Research, Inc., 1981. 46pp.

A guide for sponsoring, organizing, and managing a small group- home for three elders who cannot live alone, but do not need medical or nursing care in an institution. Appendixes give job descriptions for staff, forms and agreements, and a selected reading list.

RETIREMENT COMMUNITIES

General Works

Directories

D32. Dickinson, Peter A. *Retirement Edens Outside the Sunbelt.* New York: E.P. Dutton, 1981. xiv, 302pp.

In 1978 the author published a guide to retirement in the sunbelt. The present volume covers the rest of the country, rating communities and regions for climate, housing, employment opportunities, cost of living, taxes, medical care, cultural and recreational opportunities, and special services for seniors.

D33. Dickinson, Peter A. *Sunbelt Retirement: The Complete State-by-State Guide to Retiring in the South and West of the United States.* New York: E.P. Dutton, 1978. 338pp.

A guide and directory to retirement communities in the South and West. It uses a rating scale for such factors as climate, housing, cost of living, taxes, quality of medical care, cultural and recreational opportunities, special services for seniors, and the ethnic and political characteristics of the people.

Life Care

Directories

D34. Adelman, Nora C., comp. *Directory of Life Care Communities.* 2d ed. Kennett Square, Penn.: Kendal-Crosslands, 1980. 244pp.

A directory of life-care communities throughout the country. Each entry gives name; address; sponsorship; year established; site (rural, urban, etc.); admission requirements; resident population; charges included in fee; services available at extra charge; medical services; exclusions from medical coverage; and other data. The directory is preceded by a description of life- care communities and followed by a guide for prospective residents.

Mobile Homes

Bibliography

D35. Buchanan, Jim, and Fran Burkert. *Mobile Homes and Mobile Home Living: A Bibliography.* Public Administration Series, Bibliography no. 363. Monticello, Ill.: Vance Bibliographies, 1979. 42pp.

This bibliography on mobile homes includes ordinances regulating mobile homes. There are location and subject indexes.

INSTITUTIONAL CARE

INSTITUTIONAL CARE

Contents

INSTITUTIONAL CARE—GENERAL

General Works

Guides, Handbooks, and Manuals

E1. Brody, Elaine. *Long-Term Care of Older People: A Practical Guide.* New York: Human Sciences Press, 1977. 402pp.

Historical perspective and theoretical knowledge of long-term care, combined with how-to-do-it advice and guidance for those involved with and responsible for long-term care. Sample forms and charts are given. A bibliography is included (pp. 368- 396).

E2. Litman, Theodore J. *Syllabus on Long Term Care.* Washington, D.C.: Association of University Programs in Health Administration, 1974-1975. 3 vols.

A syllabus intended as an instructional tool for use by graduate, undergraduate, and continuing education faculty in education for long-term care administration. It includes basic orientation, institutional alternatives, and the role of the administrator in a long-term-care facility.

Statistics

E3. Palmore, Erdman. "Total Chance of Institutionalization Among the Aged." *The Gerontologist* 16(1976):504-507.

A 20-year longitudinal study of 207 normal aged-persons found that their chance of institutionalization was about one in four.

E4. U.S. Federal Council on Aging. *The Need for Long Term Care: Information and Issues.* Washington, D.C.: U.S. Government Printing Office, 1981. v, 90pp.

Charts and graphs show statistics on elders, projected through the year 2050, that have an impact on long-term care. An appendix gives the source for each statistic used.

ORGANIZATION AND ADMINISTRATION

E5. Levey, Samuel, and N. Paul Loomba, eds. *Long-Term Care Administration: A Managerial Perspective.* Health Systems Management, Vol. 10. New York: Spectrum Publications, 1977. 2 vols.

Relationship of interdependent elements of management useful for devising the best long-term care services, and a reference guide for managers of voluntary and government institutions connected with the field of long-term care. A bibliography appears in volume 2 (pp. 619-44).

Guides, Handbooks, and Manuals

E6. Brody, Elaine M., et al. *A Social Work Guide for Long-Term Care Facilities.* Rockville, Md.: National Institute of Mental Health, 1974. 216pp.

The objectives of this book are to identify the role, function, and value of social work in long-term facilities, to provide material for social work practice, to enable professionals to understand the potential of social work, and to educate and sensitize professionals who refer older people to long-term care.

E7. Corbus, Howard F., and Laura L. Swanson. *Adopting the Problem-Oriented Medical Record in Nursing Homes: A Do-It-Yourself Manual.* Wakefield, Mass.: Contemporary Publishing, 1978. viii, 98pp.

This guide directs a nursing staff through the transition from traditional medical records to the problem-oriented medical record.

E8. Miller, Dulcy B., and Jane T. Barry. *Nursing Home Organization and Operation*. Boston: CBI Publishing Company, 1979. xxvii, 454pp.

This comprehensive guide to the organization and management of a long-term care facility is profusely illustrated with photographs, diagrams, and samples of forms.

STANDARDS AND ACCREDITATION

Guides, Handbooks, and Manuals

E9. Foundation of the American College of Nursing Home Administrators. *State Licensure Requirements for Nursing Home Administrators*. Washington, D.C.: The College, 1977. 115pp. + appendix.

Abstracts, by state, of licensure requirements for nursing home administrators. Each abstract includes preexamination requirements, licensing examination requirements, reciprocity, relicensure, revocation, training and preceptor programs, board composition, and proposed changes in licensure requirements.

E10. Joint Commission on Accreditation of Hospitals. *Accreditation Manual for Long Term Care Facilities*. Chicago, 1980. xiii, 86pp.

The standards, described in 17 categories, for accreditation of long-term care facilities by the Joint Commission on Accreditation of Hospitals.

E11. Joint Commission on Accreditation of Hospitals. *Accreditation Self-Assessment Checklist for Long Term Care Facilities*. Chicago: 1980. viii, 83pp.

A categorized checklist to help nursing-home staff evaluate their facility's level of compliance with the standards contained in the 1980 edition of the *Accreditation Manual for Long-Term Care Facilities*.

Day care

Bibliography

E12. National Council on the Aging. Library. *Day Care. Demand Bibliography No. 28.* Washington, D.C.: 1977.

An alphabetically arranged bibliography, taken from the card catalog of the NCOA library and from entries in *Current Literature on Aging,* on adult day care.

Directories

E13. U.S. Health Care Financing Administration. *Directory of Adult Day Care Centers.* Comp. by Edith G. Robins and Joan Miles for the Health Standards and Quality Bureau, Health Care Financing Administration. Washington, D.C.: U.S. Government Printing Office, 1980. 162pp.

A listing by state of 618 ongoing programs that provide services to approximately 13,500 persons daily. Program information includes name, address, and telephone number of each program; director; date started; sponsoring organization; funding sources; nature of program; and average daily census. There are statistics for state program totals and sources of program funds.

Nursing homes

General Works

Guides, Handbooks, and Manuals

E14. Burger, Sarah Greene, and Martha D'Erasmo. *Living in a Nursing Home: A Complete Guide for Residents, their Families and Friends.* New York: The Seabury Press, 1976. 178pp.

A guide to choosing a nursing home, preparation for entering a home, and living in a home.

E15. Horn, Linda, and Elma Griesel. *Nursing Homes: A Citizen's Action Guide.* Boston: Beacon Press, 1977. xii, 190pp.

A report on the conditions in nursing homes and the practical steps citizen's action groups can take to improve these conditions.

E16. U.S. Health Care Financing Administration. *How to Select a Nursing Home.* Washington, D.C.: U.S. Government Printing Office, 1981. vii, 55pp.

A guide for those who must select a nursing home. It reviews the alternatives to institutionalization, provides background information on nursing homes, presents a step-by-step process for selecting a nursing home, and gives a checklist to help in the decision of selection. There are directories of state health departments, welfare departments, and nursing home ombudsman offices, and a glossary of terms used in the long-term care field.

E17. Willner, Robert F. *Criteria for Long-Term Care Placement: Referral Guidelines for the Clergy.* St. Louis, Mo.: Catholic Hospital Association, 1979. x, 31pp.

Guidelines for clergy and laymen for assessing long-term care facilities and for judging the type of facility appropriate for each prospective resident. Appendixes give checklists for evaluating facilities with a medical focus and facilities with a nonmedical focus.

Bibliography

E18. Sharma, Prakash C. *Nursing Homes and Nursing Home Administration: A Selected Research Bibliography.* Public Administration Series: Bibliography no. P 63. Monticello, Ill.: Vance Bibliographies, 1978. 8pp.

Over 100 selected references to studies on nursing homes and nursing home administration, chiefly during the period 1960-1977. Citations are listed alphabetically under books and journals.

Statistics

E19. U.S. National Center for Health Statistics. *The National Nursing Home Survey.* Vital and Health Statistics: Series 13, Data from the National Health Survey, No. 43. (DHEW Publication, No. (PHS) 79-1794). Washington, D.C.: U.S. Government Printing Office, 1979.

Data from the 1977 National Nursing Home Survey are presented in 43 tables, grouped according to facility, staff, financial, resident, discharge, and charge characteristics. Data are presented that measure utilization, staffing patterns, cost of providing care, health and functional status of residents, and discharges and payment for care.

E20. U.S. National Clearinghouse on Aging. *Human Resource Issues in the Field of Aging: The Nursing Home Industry.* AoA Occational Papers in Gerontology no. 1. Washington, D.C.: U.S. Government Printing Office, 1980. v, 20pp.

Statistics on current employment in nursing homes and projected requirements.

Residents

Guides, Handbooks, and Manuals

E21. Silverstone, Barbara. *Establishing Resident Councils.* New York: Federation of Protestant Welfare Agencies, 1974. 61pp.

Guidelines for residents and administrators desiring to organize or strengthen resident councils in residential facilities for the elderly.

HEALTH

HEALTH

Contents

F1. Burdman, Geral Dene Marr, and Ruth M. Brewer, eds. *Health Aspects of Aging*. Portland, Ore.: Continuing Education Publications, 1978. xiii, 255pp.

A book of readings on the health aspects of the aging process for health professionals and for students entering the health professions. The bibliography (pp. 241-51) includes audiovisual resources.

Periodicals

F2. *Aged Care and Services Review*. 1978. q. The Haworth Press, 149 Fifth Ave, New York, NY 10010.

Each issue contains a substantive review article of current interest, such as alternatives to institutionalization, or death and dying. The bulk of the journal consists of descriptive summaries and abstracts of over 100 recent journal articles on aged-care services.

F3. *Contemporary Administrator for Long-Term Care*. 1978. m. Contemporary Administrator, Inc, 814 South Church St, Murfreesboro, TN 37103.

Practical articles geared to nursing home administrators, news up-dates and regular features describing innovations in the various departments and services of nursing homes.

F4. *Geriatrics*. 1946. m. Lancet Publications, Inc, 4015 W 65 St, Minneapolis, MN 55435.

Although primarily a medical journal, there are articles on health care, doctor-patient relations, consumerism, the aging process, and other subjects of interest to the social gerontologist.

F5. *Home Health Care Services Quarterly.* 1979. q. The Haworth Press, 149 Fifth Ave, New York, NY 10010.

A quarterly journal with papers on home health care, including literature reviews, research papers, and papers by practitioners.

F6. *Home Health Review.* 1977. q. National Association of Home Health Agencies, 205 C St, NE, Washington, DC 20002.

The professional journal of the association featuring short, scholarly, and research articles relating to home care agency operation and patient care. Articles tend to be practical, with examples of charts, forms, and procedures. Book reviews are long and descriptive.

F7. *Journal of Geriatric Psychiatry.* 1967. s-a. International Universities Press, Inc., 315 Fifth Ave, New York, NY 10016.

Official journal of the Boston Society for Gerontologic Psychiatry. The articles are on psychiatric, psychoanalytic and psychotherapeutic aspects of old age, preceded by an introduction and followed by extensive discussion.

F8. *Journal of Gerontological Nursing.* 1975. m. Charles B. Slack, Inc., 6900 Grove Rd, Thorofare, NJ 08086.

Feature articles on nursing care and therapies for elders in various settings. There are lengthy letters from readers in response to earlier articles, news of the field in the form of short articles, a calendar covering events of interest to gerontological nurses, and descriptions of new products.

F9. *Journal of Long Term Care Administration.* 1972. q. American College of Nursing Home Administrators, 4650 East-West Highway, Washington, DC 20014.

Papers on all aspects of long-term care, geared toward the

professional workers, many written by administrators of long-term facilities.

F10. *Journal of Nutrition for the Elderly.* 1980. q. The Haworth Press, 149 Fifth Ave, New York, NY 10010.

A journal for dietitians and nutritional specialists working with elders in nursing homes, long-term care facilities, and hospitals. The journal also publishes material relevant to community programs for elders and research demonstrating the essential role of nutrition for gerontologic health care.

F11. *Journal of the American Geriatrics Society.* 1953. m. American Geriatrics Society, 10 Columbus Circle, New York, NY 10019.

Original papers, many from presentations at the annual meetings of the society, primarily on medical aspects of aging. There are also numerous articles on the aging process, the psychology of aging, health care, and social gerontology.

F12. *Nursing Homes.* 1950. bi-m. Heldref Publications, 4000 Albemarle St, NW, Washington, DC 20016.

Directed at those managing long-term care facilities, this journal addresses administration, dietetics, social services, housekeeping, and other functions in addition to implications of federal regulations and legal issues.

F13. *Social Work in Health Care.* 1975. q. The Haworth Press, 149 Fifth Ave, New York, NY 10010.

A journal to reflect the extensive activity of social workers in health care; to be an arena for exchanging ideas; for improving knowledge and skills; for augmenting and refining them; for harnessing them to have greater influence and impact on the health care systems.

Guides, Handbooks, and Manuals

F14. Abbo, Fred E. *Steps to a Longer Life.* Mountain View, Calif.: World Publications, Inc., 1979. 188pp.

A book on preventive medicine written for the layman. A bibliography appears on pages 185-188.

F15. Glickman, Stephanie, et al. *Your Health and Aging.* New York: Division of Gerontology, New York University Medical Center, 1981. vii, 213pp.

This large-type health manual for elders contains 35 sections under the categories of health care and self-help, health problems, and social services. Each section comprises an explanation of the topic, symptoms, and questions to ask a physician, self-help tips, and a glossary.

Bibliography

F16. Zarit, Steven, and Anita M. Woods, eds. *Brain Disorders in the Elderly: A Selected Bibliography.* Technical Bibliographies on Aging. Los Angeles: Ethel Percy Andrus Gerontology Center, University of Southern California, 1979. 86pp.

A bibliography, arranged by broad subject classification, selected from computerized searches of medical and other scientific literature for the period 1966-1978, and from earlier articles judged by the editors to have continuing importance.

Statistics

F17. *Facts at Your Fingertips—Almost: A Guide to Sources of Statistical Information on Major Health Topics.* Bethesda, Md.: National Center for Health Statistics, 1977.

Identifies the major areas of health interest and describes the data now available or in preparation.

F18. U.S. Health Resources Administration. DHEW Publication no. (HRA)77-628. *Health of the Disadvantaged Chartbook.* Hyattsville, Md.: 1977. 98pp.

Charts and tables giving statistics on the health status of the disadvantaged. Many of the statistics are displayed by age group.

EXERCISE

Guides, Handbooks, and Manuals

F19. Chrisman, Dorothy C. *Body Recall: A Program of Physical Fitness for the Adult.* Berea, Ky.: Berea College Press, 1980. ix, 205pp.

A guide to exercises for elders. Each exercise is completely described and illustrated and there are lesson plans for an exercise program. A bibliography is included (pp. 203-205).

F20. *Exercises While You Watch T.V.* Milwaukee: Sickroom Service, 1976. 32pp.

A booklet of exercises designed for the older or sedentary person. All may be performed while seated in a chair.

F21. Frankel, Lawrence J., and Betty Byrd Richard. *Be Alive as Long as You Live: The Older Person's Complete Guide to Exercise for Joyful Living.* New York: Lippincott and Crowell, 1980. 239pp.

Over fifty simple, easy-to-learn exercises specially designed to be done in whatever position is most comfortable. Each exercise is fully illustrated and the step-by-step directions are printed in large type. A bibliography is included (pp. 227-236).

F22. Harris, Raymond, Lawrence J. Frankel, and Sara Harris, eds. *Guide to Fitness After Fifty.* New York: Plenum Press, 1977. 356pp.

Basic and applied research data, advice, and tested techniques on physical exercise, fitness, and relaxation for older people. The book contains perspectives on exercise and age, evaluation and physiology of exercise, motivation, planning, and practical exercise and relation programs.

F23. Rosenberg, Magda. *Sixty-Plus and Fit Again: Exercises for Older Men and Women.* New York: M. Evans and Co. 1977. 142pp.

Step-by-step exercise programs developed for use in physical- fitness classes for older adults. Illustrated.

F24. U.S. President's Council on Physical Fitness and Sports. *The Fitness Challenge in the Later Years: An Exercise Program for Older Americans.* Prepared by the Council and the Administration on Aging. Washington, D.C.: U.S. Government Printing Office, 1968, reprinted 1975. 28pp.

Three exercise plans for older people, depending on their physical condition. The exercises are described and illustrated and the value of each is explained.

PHYSIOLOGY OF AGING

F25. Cohen, Stephen. "Sensory Changes in the Elderly." *American Journal of Nursing.* 81(October 1981):1851–1880.

A programmed instruction course on sensory changes associated with aging.

F26. Comfort, Alex. *The Biology of Senescence.* 3d ed. New York: Elsevier, 1979. 414pp.

The first revision since 1964 of this standard work on the aging process. It includes an extensive bibliography (pp. 333-396).

F27. Lamb, Marion J. *Biology of Ageing.* New York: John Wiley and Sons, 1977. 184pp.

A textbook that brings together some important facts and ideas about the nature and causes of the aging processes.

F28. Saxon, Sue V., and Mary Jean Etten. *Physical Change and Aging: A Guide for the Helping Professions.* New York: Tiresias Press, 1978. 192pp.

A text on the physical aspects of aging and their implications for behavior, for those who have a ' limited science background.

F29. Smith, David W., Edwin L. Bierman, and Nancy M. Robinson, eds. *The Biologic Ages of Man From Conception Through Old Age.* 2d ed. Philadelphia: W.B. Saunders, 1978. 279pp.

A textbook providing an integrated portrayal of human life from conception through old age. The changing nature of the life situation, the common disorders, and the needs for health maintenance are considered for each of the seven biologic ages of man.

F30. Thorbecke, G. Jeannette, ed. *Biology of Aging and Development.* New York: Plenum Press, 1975. 344pp.

An interdisciplinary reference book bringing together current research in the problems of development and aging from a variety of fields. It was first published in *Federation Proceedings* 34(1-2), January-February 1975.

Bibliography

F31. National Council on the Aging, Inc., Demand Bibliography no. 31. Library. *Aging Process.* Washington, D.C.: 1979. unp.

An alphabetically arranged bibliography on the physiological and psychological aspects of the aging process, taken from the card catalog of the NCOA library.

LONGEVITY

Statistics

F32. "'Gains in Longevity Continue." *Metropolitan Life Statistical Bulletin.* 59(July-September 1978):7-9.

Life expectancy through the last 50 years, and life expectancy tables for men and women for each year from birth to age 85.

DISEASES AND TREATMENT

F33. Miller, Michael B. *Current Issues in Clinical Geriatrics.* New York: Tiresias Press, 1979. xxi, 244pp.

A textbook of clinical geriatrics dealing with medical care of the institutionalized elderly.

F34. Reichel, William, ed. *Clinical Aspects of Aging: A Comprehensive Text Prepared Under the Direction of the American Geriatrics Society.* Baltimore: Williams and Wilkins, 1978. 528pp.

A compilation designed to serve as a textbook in geriatrics for continuing education, as well as undergraduate and graduate physican education, and undergraduate education of allied health professionals.

F35. Steinberg, Franz U., ed. *Cowdry's the Care of the Geriatric Patient.* St. Louis, Mo.: C.V. Mosby Co., 1976. xiv, 518pp.

A textbook of geriatric medicine with sections on medical care, surgical care, disorders of the nervous and sensory systems, geriatric rehabilitation, and special aspects of geriatric care.

HEALTH CARE

Guides, Handbooks, and Manuals

F36. *Planning and Organization of Geriatric Services: Report of a WHO Expert Committee.* World Health Organization Technical Report Series, no. 548. Geneva, Switzerland: World Health Organization, 1974. 46pp.

This report sets out the basic concepts and principles underlying the planning and organization of geriatric programs; it should serve as a useful guide for national governments and organizations interested in the provision of services for old people.

Bibliography

F37. Employee Benefit Research Institute. *A Bibliography of Research: Health Care Programs.* Washington, D.C.: 1981. Each section repaged.

A bibliography, with abstracts, summarizing research on the characteristics, costs, and utilization of health care services under current and proposed health care programs. It covers financing methods, delivery systems, and program costs of various types of health care programs. There are sections of completed research, research in progress, and information sources, with author, title, and subject indexes.

F38. Sharma, Prakash C. *A Selected Bibliographic Research Guide to Geriatric Care in Advanced Societies.* Public Administration Series, Bibliography no. 115. Monticello, Ill.: Vance Bibliographies, 1978. 8pp.

A bibliography, divided into books and journal articles, on health, health care, and longevity among the elderly.

CHRONIC ILLNESSES

Guides, Handbooks, and Manuals

F39. Soper, Michael R. *Guidelines for Chronic Care: A Team Approach.* Bowie, Md.: Robert J. Brady Co., 1977. 217pp.

Nursing guidelines for evaluation, monitoring, and shared management of ambulatory adult patients with chronic illness.

DRUG ABUSE AND ALCOHOLISM

Bibliography

F40. Barnes, Grace M., Ernest L. Abel, and Charles A.S. Ernst, comps. *Alcohol and the Elderly: A Comprehensive Bibliography.* Westport, Conn.: Greenwood Press, 1980. xvii, 138pp.

An alphabetical listing of 1,228 works dealing with alcohol consumption and the elderly population. There is a subject index with cross references.

F41. National Council on the Aging. Library. Demand Bibliography no. 32. *Alcoholism and the Aging.* Washington, D.C.: 1979. unp.

An alphabetically arranged bibliography on alcoholism and the aging, taken from the card catalog of the NCOA library and from entries in *Current Literature on Aging.*

HANDICAPPED

Guides, Handbooks, and Manuals

F42. Breuer, Joseph M. *A Handbook of Assistive Devices for the Handicapped Elderly: New Help for Independent Living.* Physical and Occupational Therapy in Geriatrics, vol. 1, no. 2. New York: The Haworth Press, 1982. 77pp.

A broad array of devices designed to assist handicapped elders toward independent living. Major emphasis is given to devices to help bedridden and elderly persons with limited strength and mobility perform daily functions by themselves.

Bibliography

F43. American Speech and Hearing Association. Committee on Communication Problems of the Aging. *Resource Material for Communicative Problems of Older Persons.* Washington, D.C.: The Association, 1975. 31pp.

An annotated bibliography of materials that can be used to acquaint patients, family members, and professionals who are not trained in audiology or speech pathology with the types of hearing, lanaguage, and speech problems commonly associated with the elderly.

F44. Russell, Martha Garrett, and Marlene Banttari, eds. *Developing Potentials for Handicaps.* Minneapolis: Home Economics Association, 1978.

An annotated bibliography and directory to program implementation for the professional involved in planning and administering programs for handicapped people, information and services for people with disabilities, and referral resources for all professionals and lay people concerned with potentials for the handicapped.

HANDICAPPED—CLOTHING

F45. Hoffman, Adeline M. *Clothing for the Handicapped, the Aged, and Other People with Special Needs.* Springfield, Ill.: Charles C. Thomas, 1979. xviii, 192pp.

Information on the provision of clothing for people with special needs, emphasizing the physically handicapped, the aged, the chronically ill, and the mentally retarded. A bibliography appears on pages 159-165.

Guides, Handbooks, and Manuals

F46. Kennedy, Evelyn S. *Clothing Changes for Special Needs.* Dressing With Pride, vol. 1. Groton, Conn.: P.R.I.D.E. Foundation, 1981. 116pp.

Twelve of the most commonly used articles of clothing, purchased at regular stores, were then modified, using special sewing methods. These simplified techniques are described in detail and clearly illustrated.

HANDICAPPED—BLIND

F47. American Foundation for the Blind, Inc. *An Introduction to Working with the Aging Person Who is Visually Handicapped.* New York: 1977. 55pp.

A source book of basic information on aging blind persons and how to work with them. It includes an extensive bibliography, and resource names and addresses are scattered throughout.

F48. Cylke, Frank Kurt, ed. *Library Service for the Blind and Physically Handicapped: An International Approach.*

International Federation of Library Association and Institutions IFLA Publications, No. 16. Munich: K.G. Saur, 1979. 106pp.

Key papers presented at the IFLA Conference, 1978, Strbske Pleso, Czechoslovakia. A directory of participants (pp. 101-106) is included.

F49. Wright, Kieth C. *Library and Information Services for Handicapped Individuals.* Littleton, Colo.: Libraries Unlimited, Inc., 1979. 196pp.

An overview of major handicapping conditions, and identification of the kinds of library services needed by handicapped individuals. Selected Organizations Providing Services to Handicapped Individuals: pp. 138-182. Directory of Selected Sources for Materials and Information on pp. 183-191.

Guides, Handbooks, and Manuals

F50. Walhof, Ramona. *A Handbook for Senior Citizens: Rights, Resources, and Responsibilities.* Baltimore: American Brotherhood for the Blind, 1981. 178pp.

A guide to tools, services, methods, and ideas for those who are going blind.

Bibliography

F51. Gibson, Merrillyn C. "Aids and Appliances for the Blind and Physically Handicapped." *HRLSD Journal.* 2(Fall 1976):15-16.

A selective bibliography compiled to assist libraries in developing their information resources on aids and appliances designed for use by the disabled.

Directories

F52. American Foundation for the Blind. *Directory of Agencies Serving the Visually Handicapped in the U.S.* 20th ed. New York: 1978. x, 437pp.

A directory listing, by state, educational services, library services, and rehabilitation services. Each entry gives name of agency, address, telephone number, director, and information on services provided. Section two gives the same information for specialized agencies and organizations. There is a large section on low vision.

F53. American Foundation for the Blind, Inc. *International Guide to Aids and Appliances for the Blind and Visually Impaired Persons.* 2d ed. New York: 1977. viii, 255pp.

More than 1,500 devices of 270 distributors in 28 countries are listed and described. Price and order information are given when known.

F54. *Large-Type Books in Print.* 3d ed. New York: R.R. Bowker, 1978. xvi, 674pp.

Author, title, and subject indexes to over 3,300 titles by 68 publishers in print which were originally printed in regular type and have been reproduced in 14-point type or larger. Each main entry gives title, series, author, coauthor, editor, translator, illustrator, grade, publication date, original publisher and publication date, binding, type size, book size, price, ISBN, imprint, and publisher. The index is in 18-point type, for use by large-type readers.

F55. U.S. Library of Congress. Division for the Blind and Physically Handicapped. *Aids for Handicapped Readers.* Reference Circular. Washington, D.C.: 1972. 17pp.

Description of reading and writing aids available for handicapped persons. Sources are listed and prices are given for most items.

F56. U.S. Library of Congress. Division for the Blind and Physically Handicapped. *Commerical Sources of Spoken Word Cassettes.* Reference Circular. Washington, D.C.: 1973. 15pp.

Under eight headings, commercial sources of cassettes are listed, giving name, address, description of the cassettes, and price. Section two gives the same information for printed sources of current information on spoken-word cassettes and equipment.

F57. U.S. Library of Congress. Division for the Blind and Physically Handicapped. *National Organizations Concerned with the Visually and Physically Handicapped.* Washington, D.C.: 1974. 14pp.

A directory of organizations offering direct services, and other associations of professional and volunteer workers who serve the needs of the handicapped or their representative organizations. Each entry gives name of the organization, address, publications, and description of services.

F58. U.S. Library of Congress. National Library Service for the Blind and Physically Handicapped. *Library Resources for the Blind and Physically Handicapped.* Washington, D.C.: U.S. Government Printing Office, 1979. vi, 108pp.

A directory of NLS network libraries and machine-lending agencies. Arranged by state, each entry gives name, address, telephone, in-WATS number, TWX number, area served, personnel, hours, and a description of the collection. Appendixes give program statistics.

HOSPITAL—OUTPATIENT SERVICES

Guides, Handbooks, and Manuals

F59. Goldsmith, Seth R. *Ambulatory Care.* Germantown, Md.: Aspen System Corp., 1977. xi, 135pp.

The organization and administration of institutionally based ambulatory care. There is a bibliography (pp. 125-130).

HOSPICES

F60. Cohen, Kenneth P. *Hospice: Prescription for Terminal Care.* Germantown, Md.: Aspen Systems Corp., 1979. xi, 302pp.

Description of hospices, history of the hospice movement, and reimbursement and legislation as they exist today. There is a glossary of terms and a directory of hospices in the U.S., Canada, and England. A bibliography is included (pp. 271-285).

F61. Davidson, Glen W., ed. *The Hospice: Development and Administration.* Washington, D.C.: Hemisphere Publishing Corp., 1978. vii, 232pp.

A report of what has occurred and what is being planned in the hospice movement in North America. There is an annotated bibliography, a discussion and list of audiovisual materials, and a directory of hospice programs in the United States.

F62. Garfield, Charles A., ed. *Psychosocial Care of the Dying Patient.* New York: McGraw-Hill, 1978. xvii, 430pp.

A book to help physicians and allied personnel identify the emotional needs of dying patients and their families, and to suggest helpful ways of providing some of the necessary support. References appear at the end of each chapter.

F63. Koff, Theodore H. *Hospice: A Caring Community.* Cambridge, Mass.: Winthrop Publishers, 1980. xii, 196pp.

The practical and theoretical principles of the hospice and the administrative, developmental, and personal elements of hospice care. A bibliography is included (pp. 181-191).

Guides, Handbooks, and Manuals

F64. Hamilton, Michael P., and Helen F. Reid, eds. *A Hospice Handbook.* Grand Rapids, Mich.: William B. Eerdmans Publishing Co., 1980. xii, 196pp.

Theoretical and practical advice on how a hospice can operate. Bibliography, pp. 181-189; Slides and Films, pp. 190-196.

F65. Zimmerman, Jack McKay. *Hospice: Complete Care for the Terminally Ill.* Baltimore: Urban and Schwartzenberg, 1981. xv, 191pp.

This guide to the organization and development of a hospice program describes the experience in the Church Hospital Hospice Care Program in Baltimore, considers the principles and practices of hospice care, reviews the composition of the hospice care team, and describes the organization, financing, and staffing of a hospice care program.

Bibliography

F66. Cook, Earleen H. *Hospices: A Bibliography.* Public Administration Series, Bibliography no. P839. Monticello, Ill.: Vance Bibliographies, 1981. 19pp.

An alphabetical listing of books and journal articles on all aspects of the hospice movement.

F67. Franklin Institute. *Hospices and Related Facilities for the Terminally Ill: Selected Bibliographic References*. Washington, D.C.: U.S. Government Printing Office, 1979. viii, 52pp.

Citations and some abstracts of publications dealing with palliative care for the terminally ill and their families, and professional treatment for the dying, primarily outside a hospital environment. Citations are listed alphabetically under Hospice Facilities; Hospice Services; Home Health Care for the Terminally Ill; and Bibliographies, Pamphlets and Newspaper Articles.

F68. Hallquist, Martha, and Robin Adame, comps. *Hospice: A Bibliography*. Denton: Center for Studies in Aging, North Texas State University, 1980. iii, 49pp.

A bibliography of 342 citations, divided among ten categories, including a section on audiovisual material. There is an author index.

HEALTH INSURANCE

F69. Commerce Clearing House. *1981 Medicare Explained*. Chicago: 1981. vi, 283pp.

A concise but thorough explanation of all aspects of the Medicare program, following the law by paragraph. There is a topical index and a durable medical equipment screening list.

F70. National Retired Teachers Association/American Association of Retired Persons. *Information on Medicare and Health Insurance for Older People*. Washington, D.C.: 1979. 25pp.

An explanation of what Medicare does and does not cover, and the respective merits, shortcomings, and relative availability of the various kinds of insurance suitable for supplementary protection.

Guides, Handbooks, and Manuals

F71. U.S. Health Care Financing Administration. *Your Medicare Handbook.* Baltimore: U.S. Social Security Administration, 1981. 61pp.

A complete guide to Medicare for insurees. There is a directory of Medicare offices by state.

EDUCATION

F72. Fasano, Marie A. *Nurse Assistant in Long Term Care: A Workbook and Instructional Program.* 2d ed. rev. Sacramento, Calif.: InterAge Publishers, 1980. 174pp.

A textbook for nurse's aides, with all procedures outlined and illustrated.

F73. Futrell, May, et al. *Primary Health Care of the Older Adult.* North Scituate, Mass.: Duxbury Press, 1980. xiv, 494pp.

A gerontological nursing textbook focusing on health promotion, prevention of illness, health assessment, and nursing management of health problems common to older adults.

F74. Walston, Betty J., and Keith E. Walston. *The Nurse Assistant in Long-Term Care: A New Era.* St. Louis, Mo.: Mosby, 1980. xiii, 204pp.

A self-help textbook for nurse's aides which describes the techniques and procedures involved in long-term care.

Guides, Handbooks, and Manuals

F75. Conahan, Judith M. *Helping Your Elderly Patients: A Guide for Nursing Assistants.* New York: Tiresias Press, 1976. 128pp.

A textbook to help nursing assistants to understand the important role they assume when caring for older people, and to increase their awareness of, and sensitivity to, the needs of elderly patients.

F76. University of Louisville, Kent School of Social Work. *Caring for the Elderly: A Workbook for Personal Care Home Aides.* Louisville: 1978. 5 units.

A manual to be used in the training of nurse's aides.

HOME CARE

Guides, Handbooks, and Manuals

F77. *Community Care Programs for the Frail Elderly.* New York: Community Service Society of New York, 1976. 102pp.

A resource guide and report based on the symposium "A Call to Action: New Ideas for Alternatives to Institutional Care for the Elderly," sponsored by the Community Service Society of New York, October 10, 1975, at the McGraw-Hill Building.

F78. Mace, Nancy L., and Peter V. Rabins. *The 36-Hour Day: A Family Guide to Caring for Persons with Alzheimer's Disease, Related Dementing Illnesses, and Memory Loss in Later Life.* Baltimore: Johns Hopkins University Press, 1981. xvii, 253pp.

A guide for home care of those in the early and middle stages of Alzheimer's disease and related disorders.

F79. Parker, Page, and Lois N. Dietz. *Nursing at Home: A Practical Guide to the Care of the Sick and the Invalid in the Home Plus Self-Help Instructions for the Patient.* New York: Crown Publishers, Inc., 1980. vi, 344pp.

A simple guide which covers the routine work necessary to provide satisfactory nursing care of a patient at home.

F80. Trocchio, Julie. *Home Care for the Elderly.* Boston: CBI Publishing Co., Inc., 1981. xi, 161pp.

A textbook and manual on home care for the aged. There are many pictures illustrating procedures and techniques.

Bibliography

F81. Home Care Information Consortium and Community Services of Pennsylvania. *Home Care Resources.* Harrisburg: Community Services of Pennsylvania, 1976. 16pp.

Listings of association, government, and university publications, audiovisual aids, journal articles, and a list of national organizations in the field of home care.

F82. National Council on the Aging. Library. *Non-Institutional Care.* Demand Bibliography no. 17. Washington, D.C.: 1975. unp.

An alphabetically arranged bibliography on problems of noninstitutional care of the aging, taken from the card catalog of the NCOA library.

F83. Sharma, Prakash C. *Alternatives to Institutional Care for Older Americans: A Selected Research Guide.* Public Administration Series, Bibliography no. 116. Monticello, Ill.: Vance Bibliographies, 1978.

A bibliography on noninstitutional care, divided into books and journal articles, and government publications.

Nurses and Nursing

F84. Carnevali, Doris L., and Maxine Patrick, eds. *Nursing Management for the Elderly.* Philadelphia: J.B. Lippincott Co., 1979. xii, 569pp.

A textbook of geriatric nursing that moves from normal to abnormal, giving perspective on the normal changes occurring in the elderly in areas significant to nursing management and high- risk health situations in older persons, together with the conceptual basis for assessment and nursing management. Bibliographies follow each chapter.

F85. Eliopoulos, Charlotte. *Gerontological Nursing.* New York: Harper and Row, 1979. x, 384pp.

An introduction to nursing care of elders. A bibliography appears on pages 357-376.

F86. Gunter, Laurie M., and Carmen A. Ester. *Education for Gerontic Nursing.* Springer Series on the Teaching of Nursing, vol. 5. New York: Springer, 1979. vii, 212pp.

A conceptual framework, delineation, and definition for a field of nursing practice and research pertaining to the nursing care of the elderly. Bibliography by chapter, pp. 193-203.

F87. Hess, Patricia A., and Candra Day. *Understanding the Aging Patient.* Bowie, Md.: The Robert J. Brady Co., 1977. 172pp.

A textbook of geriatric nursing which discusses normal aging, nursing care for the aged ill, and restorative nursing for the aged.

F88. Reinhardt, Adina M., and Mildred D. Quinn, eds. *Current Practice in Gerontological Nursing.* Mosby's Current Practice and Perspectives in Nursing Series, vol. 1. St. Louis, Mo.: C. V. Mosby Co., 1979. xvii, 237pp.

Multidisciplinary material to aid the health care provider to understand the many aspects of providing effective care and service for elders.

F89. Sultz, Harry A., O. Marie Henry, and Judith A. Sullivan. *Nurse Practitioners: USA.* Lexington, Mass.: Lexington Books, 1979. xix, 242pp.

A scholarly examination, elaboration, and dissemination of the findings of a longitudinal study of nurse practitioners, begun in 1973.

Standards

F90. American Nurses' Association. *Standards: Gerontological Nursing Practice.* Kansas City, Mo.: The Association, 1976. 8pp.

This publication sets forth standards developed by the Executive Committee of the Division on Gerontological Nursing Practice of the American Nurses' Association.

ACCIDENTS AND SAFETY

F91. National Safety Council. Home Department. *Workshop on Safety of the Aging.* Chicago: [n.d.]. 10pp.

Detailed outline of a three-day workshop on safety of the aged. Lists of films, materials, and bibliographic citations are appended.

Guides, Handbooks, and Manuals

F92. American Association of Retired Persons and National Retired Teachers Association. *Your Retirement Safety Guide.* Long Beach, Calif.: 1971. 30pp.

A guide to safety and accident prevention for older people. There are sections on crime and fraud.

F93. Lewis, Dorothea J. *Handle Yourself with Care: Accident Prevention for Older Americans.* Washington, D.C.: U.S. Government Printing Office, 1969. 18pp.

A profusely illustrated guide to accident prevention for elders, with checklists and safety rules.

F94. Pastalan, Leon A., et al. *Older Driver Refresher Course: Instructor Handbook.* Ann Arbor: University of Michigan-Wayne State University Institute of Gerontology, 1976. viii, 86+pp.

This handbook is intended to provide all the information a

professional driver-training instructor needs to teach the Older Driver Refresher Course.

Bibliography

F95. Jenkins, Antoinette, et al., eds. *Safety for the Elderly: A Selected Bibliography.* Los Angeles: Ethel Percy Andrus Gerontology Center, University of Southern California, 1975. 34pp.

A partially annotated, selected bibliography of references to safety for the elderly, taken from a keysort file of over 45,000 references. The citations are arranged alphabetically by subject.

Statistics

F96. National Safety Council. *Accident Facts.* Chicago: annual.

Statistical charts and tables on accidents in the U.S., often with multiyear comparisons. Where applicable, there is a breakdown by age.

NUTRITION

Guides, Handbooks, and Manuals

F97. *Index of Nutrition Education Materials.* Washington, D.C.: The Nutrition Foundation, 1974. 7 sections.

An index of booklets, pamphlets, and audiovisual aids to assist teachers and the general public in acquiring useful teaching aids and educational materials.

F98. Posner, Barbara Millen. *Nutrition and the Elderly: Policy Development, Program Planning, and Evaluation.* Lexington, Mass.: Lexington Books; D.C. Heath and Co., 1979. xxi, 183pp.

An analysis of the Title VII Nutrition Program for Older

Americans, quantifying program outputs and impact thus far, explaining policies, and identifying strategies for improved service delivery and goal attainment.

F99. White, Alice, Katherine A. Cooper, and Margaret C. Phillips. *A Guide for Food and Nutrition in Later Years.* Berkeley, Calif.: Society for Nutrition Education, 1976. 16pp.

A guide which discusses nutrition, shopping for food, special nutrition problems of the elderly, eating alone, and resource programs and organizations.

Bibliography

F100. Metress, Seamus P., and Cary S. Kart. *Nutrition and Aging: A Bibliographic Survey.* Public Administration Series, Bibliography no. P-309. Monticello, Ill.: Vance Bibliographies, 1979. 96pp.

An international bibliography, in 14 sections, of books and journal articles on all facets of nutrition and the elderly.

F101. Simko, Margaret D. and Karen Colitz, comps. *Nutrition and Aging: A Selected Annotated Bibliography, 1964- 1972.* DHEW Publication (SRS) 73-20237. Washington, D.C.: U.S. Government Printing Office, 1973. 41pp.

An annotated bibliography of books and journal articles on nutrition and aging, arranged under ten subject headings.

F102. Weg, Ruth B. *Nutrition and Aging: A Selected Bibliography.* Technical Bibliographies on Aging, Series 11. Los Angeles: Ethel Percy Andrus Gerontological Center, University of Southern California, 1977. 51pp.

A classified bibliography citing primarily materials on the adequacy and physiology of nutrition. Most of the citations cover the period 1969–1977, with a few selected earlier articles.

REHABILITATION

F103. Lewis, Sandra Cutler. *The Mature Years: A Geriatric Occupational Therapy Text.* Thorofare, N.J.: Charles B. Slack, Inc., 1979. viii, 183pp.

A theoretical discussion and practical guide for the study of geriatric occupational therapy.

Guides, Handbooks, and Manuals

F104. Hamill, Charlotte M., and Robert C. Oliver. *Therapeutic Activities for the Handicapped Elderly.* Rockville, Md.: Aspen Systems Corporation, 1980. xi, 295pp.

A handbook focusing on activities that are basically psychosocial and that increase the abilities of participants or improve their feelings of self-worth and independence. Part I discusses philosophy, principles, and procedures. Part II provides specific instructions for a wide range of activities, with special emphasis on their therapeutic effects for various disabilities. Bibliography and sources on pp. 255- 285.

F105. Lindner, Erna Caplow, Leak Harpaz, and Sonya Samber. *Therapeutic Dance/Movement: Expressive Activities for Older Adults.* New York: Human Sciences Press, 1979.

Guidelines and specific material to conduct therapeutic movement sessions. A bibliography appears on pages 261-267.

Bibliography

F106. Benzing, Penny. "A Selected Bibliography of Gerontology/Geriatric References for Persons in Occupational Therapy and Other Health Professions." *American Occupational Therapy Association, Gerontology Specialty Section, Newsletter.* 2(Spring 1979):1-16.

A three-part bibliography which lists, in alphabetical order, gerontology/geriatric references from *The American Journal of Occupational Therapy*—vol. 1 to vol. 32, 1947-1978; occupational therapist authored publications gerontology/geriatrics —1964—1978; and, in classified order, a selected bibliography of gerontology/geriatric references for the health professions.

MENTAL HEALTH

MENTAL HEALTH

Contents

General Works

G1. Butler, Robert N. and Myrna I. Lewis. *Aging and Mental Health: Positive Psychosocial and Biomedical Approaches.* 3d ed. St. Louis, Mo.: C.V. Mosby Co., 1982. xxii, 483pp.

A greatly revised and expanded edition of a treatise on all aspects of mental health and aging, first published in 1973. The first part is on the nature and problems of old age; the second part on evaluation, treatment, and prevention of mental illness. There are appendixes on literature sources, organizations, government programs, grant programs, and education, and glossaries on mental health and aging. There is an author index and a detailed subject index.

G2. Comfort, Alex. *Practice of Geriatric Psychiatry.* New York: Elsevier, 1980. xii, 110pp.

An overview of geriatric psychiatry and a systematic discussion of all major categories of geriatric mental disease. A bibliography is included (pp. 99-106).

G3. Isaacs, A.D., and F. Post, eds. *Studies in Geriatric Psychiatry.* Chichester, England: John Wiley & Sons, 1978. xi, 267pp.

Papers relevant to clinical work provide some of the theoretical background to the practice of geriatric psychiatry. References appear at the end of most chapters.

G4. Verwoerdt, Adrian. *Clinical Geropsychiatry.* 2d ed. Baltimore: Williams and Wilkins, 1981. xxx, 371pp.

A textbook for mental health professionals for organizing and providing mental health services for the elderly.

Guides, Handbooks and Manuals

G5. Birren, James E., and R. Bruce Sloane, eds. *Handbook of Mental Health and Aging.* Englewood Cliffs, N.J.: Prentice-Hall, 1980. xxii, 1064pp.

Original contributions by specialists from many disciplines reviewing the theory, research, and current practice of mental health and aging. Each of the 41 chapters is followed by an extensive list of references.

G6. Mace, Nancy, and Peter V. Rabins. *Family Handbook: A Guide for the Families of Persons with Declining Intellectual Function, Alzheimer's Disease, and Other Mental Dementias.* 2d ed. Baltimore: Johns Hopkins University, 1980. 71pp.

A guide for coping with the behavioral changes in a family member who is diagnosed as having dementia.

Bibliography

G7. Allen, Robert D., and Marsha K. Cartier, eds. *The Mental Health Almanac.* New York: Garland STPM Press, 1978. xix, 403pp.

Short discussions of mental health topics are each followed by an annotated bibliography of books, articles, audiotapes, and films plus, for some, a directory of information.

G8. Ciompi, L. *Geronto-Psychiatric Literature in the Postwar Period: A Review of the Literature to January 1, 1965.* Translated from the German. PHS Publication no. 1811. Washington, D.C.: Government Printing Office, 1969. 97pp.

This extensive review of the world literature on human aging contains 2,747 citations to facilitate access to reference works in clinical geronto-psychiatry and ancillary areas.

G9. Nattress, Walter K. *Gerontology and Mental Retardation: A Functional Bibliography.* Preface by John B. Balkema. Foreword by Fred J. Kraus. Harrisburg, Penn.: The Institute for Research and Development in Retardation, 1980. viii, 145pp.

A classified bibliography in three sections of 640 references, 60 percent of which are annotated. There are sections on the aging mentally retarded, general aging, and general mental retardation.

G10. Schwartz, Arthur N., ed. *Etiology of Mental Disorders in Aging: A Selected Bibliography.* Technical Bibliographies on Aging. Los Angeles: Ethel Percy Andrus Gerontology Center, University of Southern California, 1975. 51pp.

A selected bibliography, taken from a keysort file of over 45,000 references compiled from commercially available data bases and published sources, relevant to gerontology. Entries are arranged alphabetically under broad subject classification.

G11. U.S. National Institute of Mental Health. *Research on Mental Health of the Aging, 1960–1976.* Washington, D.C.: Government Printing Office, 1977. xii, 69pp.

An annotated bibliography of NIMH research relevant to the mental health problems of aging persons. Entries are listed under topic, with investigator and subject indexes.

Tests

G12. Raskin, Allen, and Lissy F. Jarvik, eds. *Psychiatric Symptoms and Cognitive Loss in the Elderly: Evaluation and Assessment Techniques.* Washington, D.C.: Hemisphere Publishing Corp., 1979. xii, 308pp.

Covers the assessment of both psychopathology and cognitive disturbances in the elderly with critical reviews of instruments used for these assessments. Extensive references follow each chapter.

G13. Schwartz, Arthur N., ed. *Assessment and Therapy in Aging: A Selected Bibliography.* Technical Bibliographies on Aging. Los Angeles: Ethel Percy Andrus Gerontology Center, University of Southern California, 1975. 58pp.

A bibliography, selected from a keysort file of over 45,000 references, of psychological tests of mental status, non-drug therapy and psychopharmacology. Most citations were published between 1959 and 1974.

PSYCHOLOGY OF AGING

G14. Botwinick, Jack. *Aging and Behavioir: A Comprehensive Integration of Research Findings.* 2nd ed., updated and expanded. New York: Springer, 1978. xi, 404pp.

A new and revised edition of a standard textbook on the psychology of aging. References appear at the end of each chapter.

G15. Eisdorfer, Carl, and M. Powell Lawton. *Psychology of Adult Development and Aging.* Washington, D.C.: American Psychological Association, 1973. 718pp.

All aspects of the psychology of the latter part of the life cycle. A bibliography appeas at the end of most papers.

Guides, Handbooks, and Manuals

G16. Birren, James E., and K. Warner Schaie, eds. *Handbook of the Psychology of Aging.* New York: Van Nostrand Reinhold, 1977. xvii, 787pp.

A handbook designed to provide an authoritative review and reference source of the scientific and professional literature on the psychological and behavioral aspects of aging. An extensive bibliography follows each chapter.

BIBLIOTHERAPY

G17. Monroe, Margaret E., eds. *Seminars on Bibliotherapy: Proceedings of Sessions June 21-23, 1978, Madison, Wisconsin.* Madison: University of Wisconsin, 1978. 180pp.

Reproduction of typescript. Papers and discussions from a seminar designed to distinguish the role of psychotherapist from that of librarian or educator in the bibliotherapeutic process and to develop a clearer picture of the relationship of mental health professionals and librarians/educators in the theory and practice of bibliotherapy.

G18. Rubin, Rhea Joyce, ed. *Bibliotherapy Sourcebook.* Phoenix, Ariz.: Oryx Press, 1978. xxi, 393pp.

The first collection in book form of articles on bibliotherapy from 1927 to the present. Appendixes give an annotated bibliography of monographs, list of theses and dissertations, and resource organizations.

Bibliography

G19. Hynes, Arleen. "Bibliography of Bibliotherapy Reference Materials 1970-1975." *Health and Rehabilitative Library Services* 1(October 1975):22-25.

A classified bibliography of materials on bibliotherapy, which includes materials from computer searches of *Psychological Abstracts, Medlars* and *Eric.*

PSYCHOTHERAPY

G20. Knight, Bob. "Psychotherapy and Behavior Change with the Non-Institutionalized Age." *International Journal of Aging and Human Development* 9(1978-79):221-236.

A literature review of psychotherapy with aged persons in the community. Includes 75 references.

G21. Sparacino, Jack. "Individual Psychotherapy with the Aged: A Selective Review." *International Journal of Aging and Human Development* 9(1978-79):197-220.

A broad review of psychotherapy and the aged. The bibliography contains 90 references.

G22. Steury, Steven, and Marie L. Blank, eds. *Readings in Psychotherapy with Older People.* Rockville, Md.: National Institute of Mental Health, 1977. vi, 223pp.

A group of papers, by leaders in the field, which highlight the utilization of psychotherapy as a method to enhance the lives of troubled older persons.

REALITY ORIENTATION

Bibliography

G23. National Council on the Aging. Library. *Reality Orientation.* Demand Bibliography no. 30. Washington, D.C.: 1977. [np]

An alphabetically arranged bibliography, taken from the card catalog of the NCOA library and from entries in *Current Literature on Aging,* on reality orientation.

PSYCHIATRIC PROBLEMS

G24. Howells, John G., ed. *Modern Perspectives in the Psychiatry of Middle Age.* Modern Perspectives in Psychiatry, no. 9. New York: Brunner/Mazel, 1981. ix, 418pp.

Comprehensive coverage of advances in developmental and clinical studies of the psychiatry of middle age. The first half of the book deals with basic theory and the second half is concerned with clinical issues.

Guides, Handbooks, and Manuals

G25. Busse, Ewald W., and Dan G. Blazer, eds. *Handbook of Geriatric Psychiatry*. New York: Van Nostrand Reinhold, 1980. xiv, 542pp.

Twenty-four papers on the biological and psychosocial bases of geriatric behavior, diagnosis, and treatment of disorders of later life, and on future directions in the field. Each paper is followed by an extensive bibliograpy.

Bibliography

G26. Gallagher, Dolores, ed. *Depression in the Elderly: A Selected Bibliography*. Technical Bibliographies on Aging. Los Angeles: Ethel Percy Andrus Gerontology Center, University of Southern California, 1981. vi, 57pp.

A bibliography of the book and journal literature from 1968 to 1980 on depression in older adults. Citations are listed under six major headings on many subheadings.

SENILITY

Guides, Handbooks, and Manuals

G27. Keane, Evelyn E., ed. *Coping with Senility: A Guidebook*. Pittsburgh: Chronic Organic Brain Syndrome Society, 1980. vi, 81pp.

A guidebook for those who are concenred with the care of a senile person. There are sections on management, therapy, nursing homes, legal problems, and death. Appendixes list organizations, agencies, and services, primarily in western Pennsylvania, but the information is germane to any locale. There is a bibliography (pp. 77-81).

RECREATION

RECREATION

Contents

RECREATION—GENERAL

H1. Moran, Joan M. *Leisure Activities for the Mature Adult.* Minneapolis: Burgess Publishing Co., 1979. vii, 184pp.

A textbook on recreation and the older adult, including background material on aging, description of sports and crafts, and the organization and programming for a recreation department.

H2. Shivers, Jay S., and Hollis F. Fait. *Recreational Service for the Aging.* Philadelphia: Lea and Febiger, 1980. xi, 324pp.

Comprehensive background for planning and presenting recreational services appropriate to the special needs, abilities, and interest of older adults.

Periodicals

H3. *Activities, Adaptation and Aging.* 1980. q. The Haworth Press, 149 Fifth Ave, New York, NY 10010.

Original, multidisciplinary articles on activities with elders. Includes articles on theory, case studies, research programming, and the effect of activities on the individual. There are evaluative book reviews and a section on resources.

H4. *Therapeutic Recreation Journal.* 1966. q. National Therapeutic Recreation Society, National Recreation and Park Association, 1601 North Kent St, Arlington, VA 22209.

Original articles on the focus, philosophy, training, program development, research, programming, and bibliography of therapeutic recreation.

Bibliography

H5. Berndt, D. Debra, and Robert O. Ray. "Leisure and the Process of Aging: Reference Points for Professional Development." *Therapeutic Recreation Journal.* 13,1(1979):50-63.

An annotated list of books, reports, conferences proceedings, public documents, and periodicals relevant to leisure, recreation, and the elderly.

H6. Mendelovitz, Lisa, and Joseph D. Teaff. *Bibliography on Recreation and Activity Programming for the Aging.* Denton: Texas Woman's University, 1975. 11pp.

An alphabetical listing of books and journal articles on recreation programming for elders. Articles come from a wide variety of journals and many different disciplines.

H7. National Council on the Aging. Library. *Leisure.* Demand Bibliography no. 27. Washington, D.C.: 1976.

An alphabetically arranged bibliography, taken from the card catalog of the NCOA library, on elders and leisure.

H8. National Recreation and Park Association. *Publications of the National Recreation and Park Association, 1981, for Park and Recreation and Leisure Services.* Arlington, Va.: 1981. 45pp.

Basically an annotated list of publications of the association, which are of interest to park and recreation personnel, educators, and lay volunteer workers. It includes some titles from other publishers. Through 1975 this catalog cited pertinent materials from all publishers.

ACTIVITY PROGRAMS

Guides, Handbooks, and Manuals

H9. Ammon, George B. *Adventures with Older Adults in Outdoor Settings: A Manual of Guidance.* Philadelphia: United

Church Press for the Cooperative Publication Association, 1972. 60pp.

A manual for leaders to determine the feasibility of outdoor activities with elders and how to establish and maintain outdoor functions in urban as well as rural settings. Although this manual is prepared for church groups, it is applicable for any leader planning activities with elders. It contains a bibliography (pp. 55-57).

H10. Barns, Eleanor K., and Herbert H. Shore. *Holiday Programming in Long-Term Care Facilities.* Denton: Center for Studies in Aging, North Texas State University, 1977. 103pp.

A guide to holidy programs that involve residents in the planning and preparation. For each of 21 holidays, the book gives a history, instructions for crafts and decorations, recipes and menus, and program suggestions. A buyer's guide to crafts and decorations, and a bibliography are appended.

H11. Bogen, Molly. *Leisure Programming for Older Adults: An Activities Guide.* Denton: Center for Studies in Aging, North Texas State University, 1981. 65pp.

An examination of initial considerations for leisure programming and a guide to activity programs in ten categories. There is a bibliography (pp. 64-65).

H12. Coster, Kathy, and Barbara Webb. *Gray and Growing: Program Packages for the Older Adult —A Manual.* Towson, Md.: Baltimore County Public Library, 1978. 113pp.

Fifteen multimedia programs designed for use by groups composed primarily of citizens age 60 and older. For each program the manual lists the materials and equipment needed, describes the content, gives an outline for use of the program, and includes an introduction, reading list, and many other materials that may be of use to the leader. Follow-up programs are suggested.

H13. Coster, Kathy, and Barbara Webb. *Gray and Growing: Program Packages for the Older Adult—A Supplement Manual.* Towson, Md.: Baltimore County Public Library, 1979. 36pp.

A supplement to *Gray and Growing,* giving guidelines for five additional program packages, a bibliography, and a list of film distributors.

H14. Cross, Gertrude. *Program Ideas for Senior Citizens.* Flint, Mich.: Flint Recreation and Park Board, 1970. 86pp.

A manual of programs and activities to be used with groups of seniors.

H15. Ross, Marilyn Heimberg. *Creative Loafing: A Shoestring Guide to New Leisure Fun.* ed. by T.M. Ross. San Diego, Calif.: Communication Creativity, 1978. 184pp.

Indoor, outdoor, and at-home activities to occupy leisure time. The book contains a bibliography (pp. 177-178).

H16. Sessoms, Robert L. *150 Ideas for Activities with Senior Adults.* Nashville, Tenn.: Broadman Press, 1977. 140pp.

Ideas for programs and projects with older people, many of them church-related. The ideas are described but, for the most part, the programs are not outlined.

H17. Spiller, Barbara. *Home Visiting Handbook of Home Activities Program: A Guide for Volunteers Who Work With the Elderly.* New York: Association YM-YWHA's of Greater New York, 1980. 50pp.

A handbook written for volunteers in a home-activities program. It outlines home visiting protocol and gives detailed instructions for five types of craft activity.

Directories

H18. Tenenbaum, Frances. *Over 55 is Not Illegal: A Resource Book for Active Older People.* Boston: Houghton Mifflin, 1979. xv, 191pp.

Directory of opportunties for people middle-aged and older, including education, volunteer opportunities, community programs, employment, and institutions. There are added sections on attitudes and physical fitness.

ACTIVITY PROGRAMS IN INSTITUTIONS

Guides, Handbooks, and Manuals

H19. Bachner, John Philip, and Elizabeth Cornelius. *Activities Coordinator's Guide: A Handbook for Activities Coordinator in Long-Term Care Facilities.* Long-Term Care Information Series. Washington, D.C.: U.S. Government Printing Office, 1978. 126pp.

A reference guide and basic textbook for those who are or are learning how to be activities coordinators in long-term care facilities. Appendices give an activities coordinator's task analysis, a long list of possible activities, guidelines for specific activities, a glossary of frequently used terms, description of common health problems of long-term care residents, a directory of national organizations and the type of help they provide, and suggested readings.

H20. Cornish, Patricia M. *Activities for the Frail Aged.* Buffalo, N.Y.: Potentials Development for Health and Aging Services, 1975. 81pp.

All aspects of working with frail elderly people are covered in this book. It outlines programs and explains activities in detail. Many mental games and activities as well as physical games and crafts are included.

H21. Desnick, Shirley G. *Geriatric Contentment: A Guide to Its Achievement in Your Home.* Springfield, Ill.: Charles C. Thomas, 1971. 61pp.

Step-by-step descriptions of programs and activities for the impaired elderly.

H22. Incani, Albert G., et al. *Coordinated Activity Programs for the Aged: A How-To-Do-It Manual.* Chicago: American Hospital Association, 1975. 158pp.

General guidelines for organizing and administering an activity department in a long-term care institution. It gives step-by-step instructions for conducting activities in such areas as arts and crafts, exercise, dance, drama, discussion groups, educational classes, entertainment, games, hobbies, music, service projects, and sports.

H23. Indiana State Board of Health. *Meaningful Activities in Nursing Homes.* Indianapolis: The Board, 1977. 64pp.

Eighty activities are listed under seven subject categories. Instructions, benefits, and supplies and equipment are given for each activity.

H24. Labanowich, Stanley, Nancy B. Andrews, and Jeanne M. Pollock. *Recreation for the Homebound Aging: Service Provider's Handbook.* Lexington: University of Kentucky, Department of Health, Physical Education and Recreation, 1978. 27pp.

The essential information necessary for selecting and conducting leisure activities in the home. It includes an analysis of selected activities and a directory of resources and resource materials.

H25. Labanowich, Stanley, Nancy B. Andrews, and Jeanne M. Pollock. *Recreation for the Homebound Aging: Trainer's Manual and Resource Guide.* Lexington: University of Kentucky, Department of Health, Physical Education and Recreation, 1978. 59pp.

Outline of a training course for personnel delivering recreation services to the homebound elderly. Appendixes contain a training resources directory and sample evaluation and assessment forms.

H26. Lucas, Carol. *Recreational Activity Development for the*

Aging in Homes, Hospitals, and Nursing Homes. Springfield, Ill.: Charles C. Thomas, 1962. 59pp.

A step-by-step approach to the recreation needs of the institutionalized elderly. There are a large number of valuable charts, forms, and resource lists helpful for starting and operating recreation programs.

H27. Merrill, Toni. *Discussion Topics for Oldsters in Nursing Homes: 365 Things to Talk About.* Springfield, Ill.: Charles C. Thomas, 1974. xvii, 235pp.

How to form and run a discussion group, topics for discussion, and questions for each topic, with a subject index.

H28. Smitley, Judy. *Creative Recreation and Socialization for Senior Citizen Centers.* Harrisburg, Penn.: City Hall, 1971. 118pp.

A manual of games and other activities for elders, to be used in senior centers or other congregate facilities. Includes chapters on group travel and camping.

ARTS AND CRAFTS

H29. Kuykendall, Terrell J., et al. *Revitalize! A Pilot Program in Arts/Aging.* St. Petersburg, Fla.: Valkyrie Press, 1979. 80pp. (Distributed by National Center on Arts and the Aging, National Council on the Aging, Washington, D.C.).

A program that incorporates the concepts behind existing programs, as well as the advice of gerontologists and experts on aging, to develop a new approach to arts programming with the aging.

Guides, Handbooks, and Manuals

H30. American Craftsmen's Council. *Crafts for Retirement: A Guide for Teachers and Students.* Ed. by Mary Lyon. New York: 1964. 134pp.

A manual for those planning a craft program for elders. The crafts described are more ambitious than those in most manuals, including such things as weaving, printing, enameling, and metalwork.

H31. Baltimore Museum of Art. *Senior Citizen Program Manual.* Baltimore: 1977. 38pp.

Guidelines for setting up programs for elders in museums. Sample evaluation forms are included to use in assessment of the program by participants.

H32. Beaubien, Joan. *Artists and the Aging: A Project Handbook.* St. Paul: Community Programs in the Arts and Sciences, 1976. 73pp.

Report on a program and guide for those who wish to establish similar programs. The goal of the program was to identify and train professional artists who would work with bringing creative opportunities to senior citizens.

H33. Gould, Elaine, and Loren Gould. *Arts and Crafts for Physically and Mentally Disabled: The How, What and Why of It.* Springfield, Ill.: Charles C. Thomas, 1978. xix, 348pp.

A guide for the craft director who works with people with many types of handicap. Over 100 craft projects are described in detail.

H34. Gould, Elaine, and Loren Gould. *Crafts for the Elderly.* Springfield, Ill.: Charles C. Thomas, 1971. vii, 210pp.

Over 75 projects are described in detail with a checklist of material that is needed. A dictionary of craft materials is included.

H35. Hoffman, Donald H. *Pursuit of Arts Activities with Older Adults: An Administrative and Programmatic Handbook.* Washington, D.C.: National Center on Arts and the Aging/ National Council on the Aging and the Center for Professional Development, University of Kentucky, 1980. 68pp.

Organization and development of arts programs with elders. Appendixes include a self-study program for professionals, a recommended book list (art library) for senior centers, a training session on arts and the isolated elderly, a directory of suppliers of visual arts materials, and a directory of state arts agencies and state aging agencies.

H36. Jones, Jean Ellen. *Teaching Art to Older Adults: Guidelines and Lessons*. Atlanta: Georgia Department of Administrative Services, 1980. 122pp.

Instructions for many arts and crafts projects for classroom use or individual instructions.

H37. Kay, Jane G. *Crafts for the Very Disabled and Handicapped: For All Ages*. Springfield, Ill.: Charles C. Thomas, 1977. xi, 205pp.

Step-by-step illustrated instructions for crafts that can be made by people who are physically or mentally handicapped.

H38. Rosenthal, Iris. *The Not-So-Nimble Needlework Book*. New York: Grosset and Dunlap, 1977. 160pp.

Detailed instructions for needlework projects designed for those people who do not have enough dexterity to use commercial kits. A directory of sources of supplies is appended.

Bibliography

H39. Jones, Jean Ellen. "Art and the Elderly: An Annotated Bibliography of Research and Programming." *Art Education*. 31, 7 (November 1978):23-29.

An alphabetically arranged, annotated bibliography covering much of the literature of visual art education and some citations from the related areas of visual perception, creativity, art therapy, leisure research, and space planning.

Directories

H40. Cahill, Pati, comp. *The Arts, the Humanities and Older Americans: A Catalogue of Profiles*. Washington, D.C.: National Council on the Aging, 1981. iii, 81pp.

Profiles of 36 arts/humanities programs used with groups of elders. Each profile gives name, sponsor, project director, history, role of sponsoring organization, objectives, content, profiles of participants, sites, organizational structure, operation, products, publicity, evaluation, funding, and contact persons.

CAMPING

Guides, Handbooks, and Manuals

H41. Armstrong, Constance H. *Senior Adult Camping*. Martinsville, Ind.: American Camping Association, 1979. iv, 46pp.

A handbook on the philosophy and operation of resident camps for senior citizens, starting with a timetable beginning eight months prior to the camping trip and including all forms, questionnaires, and lists of supplies necessary.

Bibliography

H42. Scholer, Elmer A., and Martha D. McClain. *A Selected Bibliography on Camping and Recreation for the Aging and Aged*. Iowa City: University of Iowa, Institute of Gerontology, 1968. 19 leaves.

A classified, annotated bibliography covering all aspects of camping for the elderly.

HOBBIES

Guides, Handbooks, and Manuals

H43. Chaplin, Mary. *Gardening For the Physically Handicapped and Elderly.* North Pomfret, Vt.: Batsford, 1980. 144pp.

This manual, covering all aspects of gardening for the elderly and infirm, is an American issue of a book published first in Great Britain; all of the directory information is British.

H44. Jenkins, Sara. *Past, Present: Recording Life Stories of Older People.* Washington, D.C.: St. Alban's Parish, 1978. 149pp. (Distributed by The National Council on the Aging)

A profusely illustrated description of a project wherein the author and a group of older volunteers developed a procedure for tape recording informal life history interviews with elderly people. The organization and administration of the project and the training of the volunteer interviewers are described; forms and equipment are illustrated.

H45. Koch, Kenneth. *I Never Told Anybody: Teaching Poetry Writing in a Nursing Home.* New York: Random House, 1977. 260pp.

A way to teach people who are old, ill, and institutionalized to write poetry in such a way that they like it, take it seriously, and go on writing it and getting better at it. The text is heavily illustrated with students' poems.

H46. Olszowy, Damon R. *Horticulture For the Disabled and Disadvantaged.* Springfield, Ill.: Charles C. Thomas, 1978. x, 228pp.

A guide with suggestions and procedures for initiating and conducting a horticultural program for the handicapped. An activity section lists, codes, and describes various horticultural activities. There is a bibliography of resource materials.

THEATER

H47. Morrison, Jack, et al. *Older Americans On Stage.* Washington, D.C.: American Theatre Association, 1979. 99pp.

A description of senior-adult theater as it exists across the country. Appendixes include an extensive bibliography and a "Directory of Senior Adult Theatre Groups and Resource Persons in the United States by State."

Guides, Handbooks, and Manuals

H48. Burger, Isabel B. *Creative Drama For Senior Adults: A Program For Dynamic Living In Retirement.* Wilton, Conn.: Morehouse-Barlow Co., 1980. 144pp.

A step-by-step manual for using creative drama with senior citizens. There is a chapter on adapting programs for use with the physically handicapped person.

H49. Cornish, Roger, and C. Robert Kase, eds. *Senior Adult Theatre: The American Theatre Association Handbook.* University Park: The Pennsylvania State University Press, 1981. 100pp.

A guide to different kinds of theatre programs for the elderly and a compendium of the ways in which such programs can be developed.

H50. Gray, Paula Gross. *Dramatics For the Elderly: A Guide For Residential Care Settings and Senior Centers.* New York: Teachers College Press, 1974. 59pp.

A guide with specific instructions for directing a drama group of older persons in the community or in institutional settings.

H51. Vornenberg, Bonnie L. *Enriching An Older Person's Life Through Senior Adult Theatre.* Eugene: University of Oregon, 1979. 120pp. Master's thesis.

A handbook for those initiating a senior theater program. Appendices include "Texts Relating to the Theatre," "Play

Scripts Adaptable to Senior Adult Theatre" (annotated), "Readers Theatre," "Anthologies of Plot Synopses," "Large Print Materials," "Publishers of Script Catalogues," "A Sample Play Production Time Line," and "Selected Bibliographies."

TRAVEL

Guides, Handbooks, and Manuals

H52. International Center for Social Gerontology. *The Vacation Residential Exchange Program For Older Persons: Planning Manual.* Washington, D.C.: 1977. 71pp.

A manual for developing and implementing a vacation residential exchange program for elders. It includes samples of all forms needed and suggested publicity.

H53. Weintz, Caroline, and Walter Weintz. *The Discount Guide For Travelers Over 55.* New York: E.P. Dutton, 1981. ix, 216pp.

A directory, by state, of discounts for seniors in hotels, motels, restaurants, transporation, and sightseeing and cultural attractions. The same information, but less detailed, is given for Canada, Mexico, the Caribbean, and Europe.

EDUCATION

EDUCATION

Contents

General Works

I1. College Entrance Examination Board. *350 Ways Colleges Are Serving Adult Learners.* New York: 1979. 43pp.

A classified list of 350 successful practices reported in a telephone survey of approximately 50 representative institutions.

I2. DeCrow, Roger. *New Learning For Older Americans: An Overview of National Effort.* Washington, D.C.: Adult Education Association, 1975. 150pp.

A state-of-the-art report on learning activities of older adults based on information gathered from expert informants, literatue analysis, and a questionnaire survey. There is a classified, annotated bibliography (pp. 105-150).

I3. Grabowski, Stanley, and W. Dean Mason, eds. *Education For the Aging: Living With A Purpose As Older Adults Through Education: An Overview of Current Developments.* Syracuse, N.Y.: Syracuse University, Eric Clearinghouse on Adult Education, 1974. 358pp.

A compilation of papers covering current practices in the field of education relating to aging, aimed at the practitioner. The focus is on education for aging rather than education about aging. There are references at the end of each chapter. The book is also issued by the Adult Education Association under the title *Learning For Aging.*

I4. Peterson, David A. "Educational Gerontology: The State of the Art." *Educational Gerontology.* 1(January-March 1976):61-73.

A definition of educational gerontology as education for older people, education about aging, and education of professionals. There is an extensive review of the literature and a bibliography.

I5. Sherron, Ronald H., and D. Barry Lumsden, eds. *Introduction to Educational Gerontology.* Washington, D.C.: Hemisphere Publishing Corp., 1978. xi, 308pp.

Papers from the First National Conference on Educational Gerontology in Virginia Beach, Virginia, in June 1976, together with additional studies by adult educators from colleges and universities across the country. It is designed to be used as an introductory textbook. Extensive references appear throughout.

I6. Sterns, Harvey L., et al., eds. *Gerontology in Higher Education: Developing Institutional and Community Strength.* Belmont, Calif.: Wadsworth Publishing Co., 1979. x, 293pp.

Key issues in academic gerontology and innovative approaches to the development of education, training, and research in aging. A selected bibliography of plays with gerontological themes (pp. 289-293).

I7. Weinstock, Ruth. *The Graying of the Campus.* New York: Educational Facilities Laboratories, 1978. 160pp.

An examination of educational facilities and their adaptability to the uses of elders. Included are attitudinal, programmatic, curricular, financial, and managerial considerations. The book is profusely illustrated.

Periodicals

I8. *Adult Education.* 1950. q. Adult Education Association of the U.S., 810 18th St, NW, Washington, DC 20006.

Full-length articles on research, theory, and practice of adult education, with some studies on the older adult learner. There are abstracts of adult education reports selected from materials in the ERIC Clearinghouse for Adult Education.

I9. *Educational Gerontology.* 1976. q. Hemisphere Publishing Corp., 1025 Vermont Ave, NW, Washington, DC 20005.

In the first issue, David Peterson defined educational gerontology as "the study and practice of instructional endeavor for and about aged individuals." Each issue contains articles, usually well documented, on topics relevant to educational gerontology. The section on learning resources varies with each issue, but may include evaluative book reviews, bibliographies, book lists, periodicals lists, ERIC documents, KWIC/ASTRA training resources, and government documents. There are announcements of meetings, new organizations, new services, and new journals.

I10. *Gerontology and Geriatrics Education.* 1980. q. The University of Texas Press, PO Box 7819, Austin, TX 78712.

A journal designed to serve as a forum for the exchange of curricula in gerontology and geriatrics. It contains original articles, many of them descriptions of courses of study; signed evaluative book reviews; "Programs in Gerontology and Geriatrics," a section describing selected degree programs that have significant gerontological and geriatric components; and a calendar of events.

I11. *Lifelong Learning: The Adult Years.* 1977. m (except July and August). Adult Education Association of the USA. 810 18th St, NW, Washington, DC 20006.

Practical articles reflect the interests of members of the Adult Education Association. Contains book reviews and Association news.

Guides, Handbooks, and Manuals

I12. Knox, Alan B. *Adult Development and Learning.* San Francisco: Jossey-Bass, 1977. xxi, 679pp.

A handbook which provides a selective, but comprehensive, overview of tested knowledge about adult development and learning in a form useful to practitioners. References (pp. 594-657).

Bibliography

I13. Bader, Jeanne E. "Education for Older Adults: Selected Bibliography." *International Journal of Aging and Human Development.* 8(1977-78):345-357.

An alphabetically arranged list of books, journal articles, theses and dissertations, association publications, conference proceedings, and government publications.

I14. Hammond, William, comp. *Competency-Based Adult Education Bibliography.* Upper Montclair, N.J.: Center of Adult Continuing Education, Montclair State College, 1979.

Recent curricular and research materials in the major coping skills areas such as mathetmatics, communication, citizenship, family life, health, and economics. Each entry gives full bibliographical information, address, readability or grade level of the text, and an abstract of the contents.

I15. Jacques, Joseph W., ed. *Education for Aging Bibliography.* Upper Montclair, N.J.: Montclair State College, Adult Continuing Education Center, 1975. 42pp.

A selected listing of abstracts from the National Multimedia Center for Adult Education.

I16. Michigan. University of Michigan, Ann Arbor. Institute of Gerontology. *Comprehensive Bibliography on Educational Gerontology, 1971—1972.* Ann Arbor: Institute of Gerontology, University of Michigan—Wayne State University, 1972. 20 sections.

Twenty unannotated bibliographies covering all aspects of educational gerontology. Sections vary from three to fifteen pages.

I17. National Council on the Aging. Library. *Adult Education.* Demand Bibliography No. 23. Washington, D.C.: 1976. [np]

An alphabetically arranged bibliography, taken from the card catalog of the NCOA library, on all aspects of adult education.

I18. New Jersey. Montclair State College. Department of Adult Continuing Education. *Community Education Bibliography.* Upper Montclair, N.J.: 1977. 112pp.

A classified, annotated bibliography of over 400 citations on community education, community colleges, personnel development, and media resources.

I19. Schmidt, Jeanette. *Education For Older Adults: An Annotated Bibliography.* Toronto: The Ontario Institute for Studies in Education, 1981. vi, 61pp.

An annotated bibliography arranged under nine topics, of selected resources on education for elders. It lists journal articles, reports, books, proceedings, theses, and bibliographies. Publication dates range from 1970 to 1980, with a few earlier titles of major importance.

Directories

I20. National Advisory on Adult Eduction. *National Organizations and Voluntary Associations With Adult Education Concerns in the United States.* Washington, D.C.: 1971. 39pp.

A directory providing information on intention, services, and addresses of executives of pertinent organizations on the national level.

History

I21. Portman, David N. "The Universities and the Public: A History of Higher Adult Education in the United States." Chicago: Nelson-Hall, 1979. xiii, 214pp.

An examination of the adult higher education movement in the United States, the cultural conditions that made it possible, the persons who played key roles, the characteristics that distinguished each period, and the trends that emerged and continue to the present day. A bibliography is included (pp. 195-205).

PROGRAMS

General Works

Guides, Handbooks, and Manuals

I22. Aslanian, Carol B., and Harvey B. Schmelter, eds. *Adult Access to Education and New Careers: A Handbook for Action.* New York: College Entrance Examination Board, 1980. xiii, 141pp.

A handbook to design and develop new adult career information centers in colleges and universities. There are bibliographies, resource directories, and sample forms and charts, with sections on objectives, services, career materials collection, facilities, staff, finances, marketing, and evaluation.

I23. Claeys, Russell R. *Utilization of College Resources in Gerontology: A Program Guide.* Upper Montclair, N.J.: Montclair State College, 1976. 59pp.

A program guide which illustrates the potential resources of a four-year college for use in development of programs and services to meet the needs associated with the field of gerontology.

I24. Hendrickson, Andrew, ed. *A Manual on Planning Educational Programs For Older Adults.* Tallahassee, Fla.: Florida State University, Department of Adult Education, 1973. 178pp.

A general guide for those wishing to initiate educational programs for the aging.

I25. Korim, Andrew S. *Older Americans and Community Colleges: A Guide for Program Implementation.* Washington, D.C.: American Association of Community and Junior Colleges, 1974. 126pp.

A guide for the expansion of community college participation in the total system of services to the elderly. Appendixes list courses for degree programs and give course outlines.

I26. Scanlon, John. *How to Plan a College Program For Older People*. New York: Academy for Educational Development, 1978. vi, 113pp.

A manual, prepared for colleges and universities, on how to plan, organize, and finance academic programs for older people.

I27. Schwartz, B., ed. *Utilization of College Resources in Gerontology: A Program Guide*. Upper Montclair, N.J.: Montclair State College, 1976. unp.

A presentation that gives guidelines for use by four-year colleges in implementing gerontology programs to provide educational and training services to community agencies serving the elderly.

I28. Utah. University, Salt Lake City, Rocky Mountain Gerontology Center. *Education and Training in Aging: A Practical Guide for Professionals*. Salt Lake City: 1975. 149pp.

A collection of papers for use by educators, trainers, and others responsible for developing short-term educational programs in the field of aging. The articles are practical tools, with concepts and suggestions for designing conferences, workshops, and short courses on aging. Ideas are applied rather than theoretical. Bibliographies are included (pp. 91-102).

Directories

I29. American Association of Community and Junior Colleges. *Older Americans and Community Colleges: An Overview*. Washington, D.C.: 1974. 35pp.

A summary of programs for elders in community colleges and the following directories, by state: 1. Community College Manpower Training Programs for the Field of Aging,

2. Retired Senior Volunteer Programs in Community and Junior Colleges, 3. Retirement Education Programs Offered in Community and Junior Colleges, 4. Cultural Enrichment Courses for Senior Citizens in Community and Junior Colleges, 5. Community and Junior Colleges That Offer Free or Reduced Tuition for the Elderly.

I30. *Catalog of Adult Education Projects.* Washington, D.C.: National Clearinghouse for Adult Education and Lifelong Learning, annual.

A catalog divided into three sections: project summaries, a series of matrices, and a subject index. The summaries are arranged alphabetically by state.

I31. Elderhostel, Inc. *1981 Summer Catalog.* Newton, Mass.: annual. 87pp.

Elderhostel is a network of over 400 educational institutions in 50 states, Canada, Great Britain, Denmark, Sweden, Finland, and Norway which offer special low-cost, short-term residential academic programs for older adults. The 1981 catalog describes 927 weeks hosted by 406 institutions in the United States and Canada. Institutions are listed by state or province, and descriptions of courses and expenses for each are given.

I32. Florio, Carol. *Collegiate Programs for Older Adults: A Summary Report on a 1976 Survey.* New York: Academy for Educational Development, 1978. 52pp.

A summary of a research study of collegiate programs for older adults. The appendixes give a directory, arranged by type of program, of institutions that have elders programs, a summary of state educational policies providing free or reduced tuition, characteristics of 107 programs, a list of courses taken by older adults, and the most popular courses among elders.

I33. Lumsden, D. Barry, Betsy M. Sprouse and Donald W. Hartley. *Catalog of U.S. and Canadian Correspondence Instruction on Aging.* Richmond: Virginia Commonwealth University, 1976. 21pp.

Courses are listed and described by subject and institutions; addresses are listed by state of province.

I34. Sullivan, Ellen Newmyer, ed. *National Directory of Educational Programs in Gerontology.* 3d ed. Washington, D.C.: Association for Gerontology in Higher Education, 1981.

A directory of 169 institutions that are members of the association. For each institution is given director, address, telephone number, degree and certificate programs, courses, short-term education/training, special opportunities for older adults, research activities, resources and services, special information, and contacts for further information. This directory does not supersede the first edition, which listed all programs, including nonmember institutions. The second edition describes some programs that have subsequently dropped membership and are thus not in this volume.

Tuition

I35. Long, Huey B. "Characteristics of Senior Citizens' Educational Tuition Waivers in Twenty-One States: A Follow-Up Study." *Educational Gerontology* 5(April-June, 1980):139-149.

The extent to which senior adults have enrolled in postsecondary educational institutions through the provisions of tuition-waiver programs, as reported in a survey of the 21 states identified as having statewide legislation or policies concerning tuition-waiver programs.

I36. Long, Huey B., and Boyd E. Rossing. "Tuition Waivers for Older Americans." *Lifelong Learning: The Adult Years.* 1(June 1978):10-13.

A report on the states in which older citizens may enroll in public higher education institutions without paying tuition, or with significant reduction in tuition fees.

CURRICULA FOR JUVENILES

I37. Pratt, Francis E. *Teaching About Aging.* Boulder, Colo.: Social Science Education Consortium, 1977. iii, 75pp.

Covers issues of aging in American society as they relate to the various disciplines in the social sciences, strategies for dealing with the issues in social studies, and recommended resources for teachers and learners.

Guides, Handbooks, and Manuals

I38. Cameron, Marcia J. *Views of Aging: A Teacher's Guide.* Ann Arbor: Institute of Gerontology, The University of Michigan- Wayne State University, 1976. 179pp.

Guides teachers in developing a unit on aging in schools and in incorporating materials on aging in the courses of many disciplines.

I39. Jantz, Richard K., et al. *Children's Attitudes Towards the Elderly: Curriculum Guide.* College Park: Center on Aging, University of Maryland, 1976. 64pp.

A resource for classroom teachers of children ages 3-11 which includes a rationale and justification for developing positive attitudes in children toward the elderly and the aging process, suggested goals, and specific objectives and activities designed to foster these goals for each age-level concerned. Resources for teachers and children are included.

LIBRARIES

I40. Bagnell, Prisca von Dorotka, ed. "Gerontology and Geriatrics Collections." *Special Collections.* 1(3/4): entire issue (In Press)

Seen only in uncorrected galleys, this volume of *Special Collections* illustrates the diversity of information resources in the field of aging, the interdisciplinary nature of the subject and the complexity of a systematic literature search.

Directories

I41. Franklin Research Center. *Guide to Selected Information Resources in Aging*. Washington, D.C.: U.S. Administration on Aging, 1980. 95pp.

A compilation of three directories—Clearinghouses, Data Bases and Information Centers; Federal Agencies and Other Federal Units Which Administer and Support Programs for Older Americans; and Gerontological Organizations. This is followed by an appendix which is a directory of state agencies on aging and the regional offices of the U.S. Administration on Aging.

I42. 1979 Gerontological Librarians/Libraries. *Gerontological Librarians' Newsletter*. 3(1979):Supplement.

Seventy-two addresses of collections, librarians, and others responsible for the collection and dissemination of gerontological literature. The entries are listed alphabetically by name, so to use it as a place indicator the whole list must be scanned, but with such a brief directory this can be done without difficulty.

I43. Owens, H. Jean. *Directory of Gerontological Libraries and Information Centers*. Detroit: Wayne State University—University of Michigan. Institute of Gerontology, 1980. xiii, 77pp.

A directory of libraries, information centers, special and private collections in gerontology, and gerontology collections within college and university libraries. Entries are arranged according to state, each entry including institution and address, name of library or collection, name of librarian or contact person, nature of the collection and library profile. Indexes provide access by the name of the institution, librarian or contact person, and subject.

LIBRARY SERVICES

I44. American Library Association. Office for Library Outreach Services. *How Public Libraries Serve the Aging.* Chicago: 1981. 234pp.

A sampling of over 150 outreach services being offered to the aging in the libraries of 29 states. For each program, the book gives a program description, title, location, contact person, clientele, purposes and objectives, staff, staff development and training activites, advisory committee, beginning of program and sources of funding, content areas, materials collections, materials developed for the program, collaborative agencies, and results.

I45. Bramley, Gerald. *Outreach: Library Services for the Institutionalized, the Elderly, and the Physically Handicapped.* Hamden, Conn.: Linnet Books, 1978. 232pp.

For each type of specialized reader, the history of library service is traced both in the United States and the United Kingdom. This is followed by a treatment of organization and administration of libraries in institutions, and methods of library service to the homebound and the disabled. A bibliography appears on pages 218-226.

I46. Library and Information Services for Older Adults. *Drexel Library Quarterly.* 15(April 1979):1-91.

An entire issue devoted to many facets of library services to seniors. The papers are: Casini, Barbara P., and Joan Appel. "Some Introductory Remarks on Library and Information Services for Older Adults (pp. 1-4); Robinson, Wendy. "Meeting the Psychological and Social Needs of Older Adults: The Library's Role" (pp. 5-19).; Fischer, Mary Wood. "The Needs of Older Adults: Materials and Access" (pp. 20-28); Balkema, John B. "Interagency Cooperation for Service to Older Adults" (pp. 29-42); Webb, Barbara. "Gray and Growing: Programming with Older Adults" (pp. 43-59); Luck, Carolyn. "Information and Referral Service for Older Adults" (pp.

60-70); Monroe, Margaret E. "Continuing Education for Older Adults" (pp. 71-82); Farina, Vibiana. "Library and Information Services for Older Adults: An Annotated Bibliography" (pp. 83-91).

I47. McClaskey, Harris C., ed. "Institution Libraries." *Library Trends* 26(Winter 1978):301-446.

This issue discusses library users within institutions, their needs and the responses of librarians and libraries to those needs. The papers are: McClaskey, Harris C. "Introduction" (pp. 301-305); Duplica, Moya M. "The Users of Institution Libraries" (pp. 307-317); Parks, Lethene. "The Library in the Institution" (pp. 319-340); Drennan, Henry T. "Institutional Libraries: Federal Perspectives" (pp. 341-360); Kinney, Margaret M. "The Institutionalized Adult's Needs for Library Service" (pp. 361-369); Matthews, Geraldine M. "The Institutionalized Child's Needs for Library Service" (pp. 371-387); Hinseth, Lois. "Materials and Collections" (pp. 389-412); Lucioli, Clara E. "An Overview of Public Library Services" (pp. 413-429); Casey, Genevieve M. "Education for Institutional Library Service" (pp. 431-445); and "List of Acronyms" (p. 446).

I48. Phinney, Eleanor. *The Librarian and the Patient: An Introduction to Library Services for Patients in Health Care Institutions.* Chicago: American Library Association, 1977. 352pp.

An introduction to the basic principles of librarianship, as applied to patient care, that are essential in any situation in which the librarian is servicing the patient.

Guides, Handbooks, and Manuals

I49. Guidelines for Library Services to an Aging Population. *RQ.* 14:237-239 (Spring 1975).

Guidelines drawn up by the Committee on Library Services to an Aging Population of the American Library Association (RASD) to encourage libraries to keep pace with the increased national interest in the special needs and problems of persons over age 65 and to respond to an expressed need by librarians who are seeking ways to initiate and develop services to this growing segment of the population.

I50. Jeffries, Stephen R. *A Model for Service to the Elderly by The Small/Medium Sized Public Library*. Denton: North Texas State University, Center for Studies in Aging, 1978. iv, 79pp.

Background of library service to elders, guidelines for developing programs, and bibliographies and directories of sources and resources for initiating and continuing programs.

Bibliography

I51. Weiss, Ina J. *Libraries—Services to the Aged: A Bibliography*. Exchange Bibliography no. 1433. Monticello, Ill.: Council of Planning Librarians, 1978. 11pp.

A bibliography of books, journal articles, government documents, and reports published between 1970 and 1977 on library services to the aged.

I52. Weiss, Ina J. *Libraries—Services to the Disadvantaged: A Bibliography*. Public Administration Series Bibliography no. 21. Monticello, Ill.: Vance Bibliographies, 1978. 18pp.

A bibliography of books, journal articles, reports, bibliographies, government documents, and pamphlets published from 1970 to 1977 that brings together references on library service to the disadvantaged.

NAME INDEX

SUBJECT INDEX